THE YEAR

THE YEAR

An Ecology of the Zodiac

SPIKE BUCKLOW

REAKTION BOOKS

Dedicated to Tara, Ella and Isabelle

Published by
REAKTION BOOKS LTD
Unit 32, Waterside
44–48 Wharf Road
London N1 7UX, UK
www.reaktionbooks.co.uk

First published 2025
Copyright © Spike Bucklow 2025

EU GPSR Authorised Representative
LOGOS EUROPE, 9 rue Nicolas Poussin, 17000, La Rochelle, France
email: contact@logoseurope.eu

Printed and bound in Great Britain by Bell & Bain, Glasgow

A catalogue record for this book is available from the British Library

ISBN 978 1 83639 078 7

CONTENTS

Design based on decorative element in Andreas Cellarius' *Harmonia Macrocosmica* (1661).

Ecology and the Zodiac

This book is about how nature keeps changing through time. Those changes repeat but, paradoxically, are never the same. Nature's shifting qualities are what sustain life and, importantly, those qualities are reflected in our own natures. Whether we were born in the city or the country, among mountains, on plains or by the sea, we are all shaped by our environments and, in turn, they were shaped by the passing of time.[1] Today, artificial light, central heating and long-haul flights have weakened our connections with nature, yet seasonal affective disorder (SAD), flu and jetlag show that we are still intimately linked to the natural world's rhythms. And, hidden deep in our DNA, about a quarter of our genes still vary their activity through the year. No one knows why.[2]

For well over 3,000 years the Western world has measured time's passing with four seasons. Of course, the four seasons are not universal. Widely spread Indigenous cultures across Australasia, for example, recognize between two and nine seasons, but here we will focus on how time's rhythms have been felt across Europe, the Middle East and most other temperate zones. And, according to the poet John Keats, each of us who lives through those four-part years participates in that same pattern. We have our seasons; being 'lusty' in life's springtime, 'dreaming high' in summer and 'contented' in our autumn, before enduring a winter of 'pale misfeature' (*The Human Seasons*). Like nature, we change but also remain the same.

This book considers the different ways in which nature expresses the passage of time through the qualities of spring, summer, autumn and winter. These four seasons are quite distinct but, thousands of years ago, people fine-tuned them with twelve months, so that each season's story had a beginning, a middle and an end. The following chapters consider those twelve qualities. Much evidence comes from the recent findings of science, mainly from ecologists who study minute details in life's interconnected web. Yet the book also draws on historical evidence, acknowledging that those who studied nature in the ancient to early modern worlds were equally sharp-eyed.[3]

Of course, the seasons are governed by the Earth's relationship with the Sun, which seems closer in the summer and more distant in winter.[4] So, spotting seasonal patterns has always involved linking the behaviour of things on Earth to the behaviour of things – like the Sun and Moon – in the heavens. This is a central aspect of what is now called 'cultural astronomy' and was a key contributor to what has become known as 'traditional ecological knowledge'.

The importance of traditional ecological knowledge is now acknowledged by modern sciences like ethnopharmacology, the discipline that turns Amazonian herbal remedies into anti-cancer drugs, for example. But that recognition has come very late in the day because much traditional ecological knowledge – as well as the Indigenous cultural astronomy that underpins it – is now seriously endangered or completely lost. For example, on Rapa Nui or Easter Island, astronomical and other cultural records were carved on wooden tablets, the overwhelming majority of which were burned in systematic campaigns intended to eradicate local knowledge. Luckily, Europe's cultural astronomy – and its other Indigenous sciences – fared much better. From the seventeenth century onwards, modern science merely plundered and repackaged bits of them, then marginalized the rest.[5]

So, before looking at each of the twelve months in turn, this Preface briefly outlines how our modern understanding of time was shaped by a key part of our own – largely dismissed – Western cultural astronomy, the zodiac. It will also suggest how the ancient zodiac can provide a broad context that complements detailed modern ecological field-studies.

European cultural astronomy grew out of millennia of Babylonian observations of how the Sun, Moon, planets and stars moved across the sky. Sometime before 1100 BC the year was divided into months and, sometime before 400 BC, the stars on the ecliptic – the Sun's path across the sky – were grouped into twelve constellations of equal length.[6] These became the zodiac signs, each of which took two hours to appear and disappear across horizons. Twelve solar months – each of around thirty 24-hour days – enabled the coordination of public events and sophisticated agriculture. Cuneiform tablets from around 400 BC show that Babylonians also had personal horoscopes based on birth signs. Luckily, those tablets were not like the wooden ones that went up in smoke on Rapa Nui. They were made of clay, so, when buildings were razed to the ground, they were accidentally fired and survived.

BY ABOUT 550 BC, the Greeks had acquired Babylonian star-lore and, a century later, it became more accessible through a poem by Aratus, who simply translated Babylonian names for the constellations. The Greeks also adopted some aspects of Egyptian cultural astronomy and, in a crucial innovation around 150 BC, Hipparchus merged the combined schemes with centuries of Greek observations. He noted a relationship between the signs of the zodiac and four key times in the year; the longest and shortest days (the summer and winter solstices) and the times when the day and night were of equal length (the spring and autumn equinoxes). Focusing on those four special days, Hipparchus spotted a pattern and used it to radically reshape Greek cultural astronomy.

Using historic records, Hipparchus related the solstices and equi-noxes to the zodiac signs and found that the occurrence of those special days shifted by about three days every two hundred years. This gradual movement of the stars with respect to the Earth – now called the precession of the equinoxes – means that the constellations slowly circulate, almost realigning approximately every 26,000 years. (There are even bigger cycles of time. A Hindu tradition has innu-merable periods of over 4 billion years – *kalpas*, or days of Brahma, alternating with equally long nights – each divided into *manvantaras* and *yugas*.) Along with other traditions, the ancient Greeks had sequences of Gold, Silver, Bronze and Iron Ages, names which sug-gest changes in the quality of time – like four seasons – possibly through what Plato called the Perfect or Great Year of about 36,000 solar years (*Timaeus* 39d).

At a speed of three days every two hundred years, each solstice and equinox takes about 2,150 years to move through a zodiac sign. And, since there is relative movement between the solstices and equi-noxes and the constellations, we can choose to define time either by those four special days or by the twelve signs. Babylonian cultural astronomy was 'sidereal' and defined time by the constellations, let-ting the solstices and equinoxes slowly drift through time. This accommodates vast cycles like the Hindu *yugas* and mythical Greek Ages. On the other hand, Hipparchus chose to define time with sol-stices and equinoxes, letting the zodiac signs slowly drift through time. This 'tropical' style of cultural astronomy loses track of cosmic time's slow rhythms and privileges our much briefer experience of time on Earth. It is the origin of the modern fixed seasons, months and weeks, and even our hours, minutes and seconds.

European cultural astronomy therefore developed around four fixed dates, defining four distinct seasons. The spring equinox kicks off springtime, when daylight dominates and days are lengthening. The summer solstice starts summertime, when daylight still domi-nates but days are shortening. The autumn equinox introduces autumn, when days continue to shorten, and the night dominates. The winter equinox initiates winter, when night still dominates but the days start lengthening again. Each of these four seasons consists of three months; a 'cardinal' one that opens the season; a 'fixed' one at the middle, in which the season has fullest expression; and a 'mutable' one which draws it to a close, preparing for the next. (A Glossary at the back of the book defines some less familiar terms.)

This way of tracking the passage of time is obviously relevant to the natural world and agriculture since plants and animals all respond to the changing length of days. But it may not seem so relevant to modern ways of life that seem insulated from the seasons. However, connections are still there. For example, in the century before Christ, Julius Caesar established the 365¼-day calendar which started on the spring equinox. However, the solar year is not exactly 365¼ days and, after about 1,600 years, the calendar had slipped 10 days behind the Sun. Pope Gregory XIII therefore shifted the calendar to catch up with the Sun and the British eventually followed. So, thanks to Julius and Gregory, the British tax year now starts just after the spring equinox, as if government coffers start swelling when sap starts rising. The calendar year itself now starts just after the winter solstice, the time of greatest darkness when light re-enters the world, which is, of course, a cosmically appropriate time for the birth of Christ, as the 'light of the world'.[7]

IN THE MODERN world, time is said to flow in a straight line, but the zodiac treats time as cyclic, which is entirely appropriate for understanding nature's seasons and agriculture. In fact, the word 'zodiac' means 'circle of little animals', which suggests a possible connection with the modern science of ecology. Immediately, though, it must be admitted that the zodiac and ecology might initially seem strange bedfellows. After all, the zodiac is now associated with astrology, which some dismiss as a pseudo-science. A little historical perspective, however, shows that they may not actually be quite such strange bedfellows, after all.

To many people today, some of the zodiac may look like science (astronomy) and some may look religious (pagan). But that is only because, since the nineteenth century, we have grown used to the idea of science and religion being somehow disconnected. For ancient cultural astronomers, there was absolutely no separation between what we now call science and religion. They were just trying to understand God and their place in the universe, in exactly the same way that the forerunner of modern science, Sir Isaac Newton, dedicated his life to diverse studies of God's creation. Of course, different people's understandings of God took different forms, so cultural astronomies also differed. Nonetheless, globally, all cultural astronomers sought to deepen their understanding of how we all fit into the universe. The modern idea of a pseudo-science – itself a denial of modern science's own roots – fails to recognize that most traditional European sciences and global Indigenous sciences were essentially religious.[8] By being simultaneously both religious and scientific, those 'natural philosophies' were able to accommodate paradoxes such as the fact that, while time can 'fly', it can also 'drag'. Indeed, one of the ways the traditional zodiac complements modern ecology is by reconciling the difference between science's uniform clock-time and the many varieties of lived-time that we all experience. And nature demonstrates how lived-time's many different qualities – flying, dragging and more – can all coalesce into an extraordinarily graceful, orderly dance.

The assumptions, methods and aims that underlie the zodiac are those of a traditional science, and they differ from the assumptions, methods and aims of modern science. But, within their own realms, both types of science – traditional and modern – are valid. The zodiac provides the book's backbone because it willingly embraces the ambiguities and paradoxes that evade modern science. And ecology puts meat on that backbone because, as a discipline, it takes all the tools that modern science has developed to look at apparently separate things and then, subversively, uses them to reconstruct connections between those things.

WE ALL POSSESS SOME imagination and some intuition. We all use logic and reason. So, the combination of the zodiac and ecology can potentially speak to both sides of us. Together, I hope that the apparently odd couple – the traditional zodiac and modern ecology – can hint at the depth of our connections with nature and our own ever-shifting place in the world. Rediscovering those connections can go towards helping heal the rifts that currently complicate our relationships with nature, including our own human nature.

The outward rift between us and nature reflects an inner rift that started opening in thirteenth-century Europe. By the eighteenth and nineteenth centuries, the fissure had become very obvious indeed. Then, a poet like William Wordsworth could draw his ideas about nature from watching the behaviour of wandering clouds ('Daffodils'), while an engineer like James Watt could draw his very different ideas about nature from studying the behaviour of trapped steam. In their own ways, those different conceptions of nature were both correct and, eventually, they made steam trains that took tourists to the Lake District. Yet beneath them, echoing the split between science and religion, the paths of engineering and poetry were diverging dramatically.

Strictly speaking, Wordsworth's wandering clouds weren't lonely. They were not distinct individuals. They could merge together and they could dissolve. Nonetheless, the poetic image has an undeniable romantic power, a power that comes from anthropomorphism. And precisely because anthropomorphism has power, it also has dangers, not the least of which is – perhaps surprisingly – limiting our imagination. For example, like us, dolphins have languages and crows use tools, so anthropomorphism helps us see them as intelligent beings. But, to us, mould and fungi don't even seem to have heads or brains, so how could they possibly be intelligent? Yet they are indeed intelligent, and they demonstrate it by sensing their world, exploring it, making decisions and solving problems. Without their completely alien intelligence they would not survive and we – who utterly depend on them – would all be dead too.

On the other hand, if Wordsworth's anthropomorphized poetic ideas about nature are not literally true then, in stark contrast, the nature of Watt's condensing steam actually *is* literally true. But it can only be true because the situation he was imagining – inside an engine's piston – is totally *un*natural. A piston engine is a very simple thing, totally divorced from the complexities of raw nature. Natural phenomena are far too complicated to be captured by any unambiguous scientific facts. As Homer, Dante and Shakespeare knew, nature's richness exhibits multilayered truths that can only be approached through analogy. Now, at the dawn of the Anthropocene, we can see the consequence of taking two separate paths, neither of which can completely accommodate nature's fullness. The divorce of Wordsworth's and Watt's different views of nature is proving catastrophic.

Poetry and reason have only recently become seen as an odd couple, and perhaps reuniting them – or ancient myth and modern science – can help us learn to live with a nature that is riven with ambiguity and paradox. After all, steam can both wander (as a lonely cloud) and be propulsive (trapped in a piston). Nature is also extremely delicate while being incredibly resilient. The combination of modern science and ancient myth may also help us come to terms with a nature that is not separate from culture but always has been, and always will be, intimately entwined with us. In mythical terms, nature is both Apollonian and Promethean, or orderly and comprehensible, as well as Dionysian and Orphic, or chaotic and incomprehensible. In Shakespeare's terms, nature is both the forest of *As You Like It* and the weather of *King Lear*.

THIS BOOK IS about how nature unfolds through time. It approaches nature – as understood by the modern science of ecology – and complements it with an understanding of nature – including human nature – as suggested by premodern European cultural astronomy. At its heart is the feeling that purely modern scientific and purely mythic approaches to nature are both unbalanced. Today, a healthy balance can only be achieved by acknowledging both nature's scientific and mythic sides. The book also attempts a balance between our actual experience of nature and an exploration of nature's laws.

Yet, as an expression of law, how does the mythical zodiac understand nature? Very briefly, the traditional European (Aristotelian and Neoplatonic) science that underlies the zodiac sees (personified) Nature as the relationship between a constant Realm of Being (the heavens) and a changing Realm of Becoming (everything under the Moon). In this Realm of Becoming, changes happen because everything (animal, vegetable, mineral, elemental and human) participates (in both harmony and conflict) in an enigmatic journey from imperfection to perfection. That journey unfolds completely naturally since all things wish to express themselves, following the models provided by the Realm of Being. So, fire always rises and water always falls, while fish swim and birds fly. However, nature's journey is not limited by any single law, so some fish can fly and some birds can swim.

And, of course, the end of nature's journey is shrouded in mystery. We all know that 'time passes' but none of us knows 'where it goes'. Also, a journey's end assumes a linear view of time, from creation to destruction or from birth to death. On the other hand, the zodiac's cyclic view of time offers an alternative story; not one of creation and destruction but one of preservation, where preservation is the interplay of the countless births and deaths that sustain life.

Creation, preservation and destruction all take place through time. A tree *exists* in space, but the things it *does* – growing, housing birds, decaying, feeding beetles and so on – happen in time. Giving time a linear shape – a now-secularized Christian innovation – lends stories a narrative arc and helps oil the wheels of industry. But giving it a circular shape helps accommodate life's vicissitudes. For example, after the summer solstice – the longest, warm and light, day – life is easy, while around the winter solstice – the shortest, cold and dark, day – life is more difficult. Around the spring equinox – as days grow and nights shrink – life is full of hope and promise, while around the autumn equinox – as days shrink and nights grow – life is full of either contentment or trepidation, depending on whether or not harvests have been good. The cycle of the seasons (in this changing Realm of Becoming) reflects the cycle of the heavens (the constant Realm of Being), which contains all possibilities. And, according to Plato, what we experience as time is merely the 'moving image of eternity' (*Timaeus* 37d).

ANCIENT CULTURAL ASTRONOMY studied heaven's order because following the stars helped 'going with the grain' of the universe, rather than struggling 'against the grain', like sowing and harvesting when 'the time is right'.[9] But, in his *Timaeus* – a book that inextricably entwined science and religion, or reason and poetry – Plato said that by following the 'unvarying revolutions' of the stars we could also stabilize the 'variable revolutions' within ourselves (47c–d).[10] He seemed less interested in using the stars to regulate agriculture and more interested in using them to help us navigate our own inner, personal journeys.

The journey this book will take is quite ordinary and, at the same time, completely extraordinary, like a pilgrimage. While ordinary journeys start somewhere and end somewhere else, pilgrimages start in the everyday world and end in sacred space. Europe is criss-crossed by shared pilgrims' paths – from Santiago de Compostela in the west to Trondheim in the north – and private pilgrimages took place everywhere, leaving absolutely no physical trace. For example, people who wandered through the world – like a lonely cloud? – with no apparent purpose were said to 'saunter'. According to Thoreau the word came from the French *sainte-terre*, or Holy Land, the place they were supposedly heading to or, perhaps, where they were coming from. Thoreau's interpretation of the word is poetic, but it is also in accord with the word's widely accepted fifteenth-century origin in *santren*, which means to muse upon, or be in a reverie.

Reveries and musings remind us that journeys need not be through space. But – whether taking place in the outside world or in the mind – all journeys move through time. As Keats said, the year's unfolding mirrors our own unfolding, and the following chapters will saunter through, or muse upon, the twelve months. Chaucer started his fictional pilgrimage 'When the sweet showers of April have pierced/ The drought of March, and pierced it to the root' (*The Canterbury Tales*), so we will also start then, at the beginning of spring. We will go from a time of hope and promise, to one of ease. Then on to a time of contentment or trepidation, to one of hardship. Then back, once again, to a time of hope and promise.

Aries, based on star chart in Andreas Cellarius' *Harmonia Macrocosmica* (1661).

ONE

March–April
Cardinal Fire, 'Emergence'

In the Western world, the calendar starts around the middle of the twelve days of Christmas, which is about ten days after the winter solstice, the time of the shortest day and longest night. However, in nature, the year seems to start around the spring equinox, when the day and night are equally long, when days are growing and nights are shrinking. In the Christian tradition, the first of those beginnings was marked by the birth of Christ, while the second is linked to his death and resurrection. These two possible start-dates connect the material and the spiritual worlds, and both are determined by the Earth's relationship with the heavens, in particular, Earth's connection with the Sun. The first, calendar start, comes after Earth's – or, to be more precise, the northern hemisphere's – six-month descent into darkness turns into the six-month ascent into light. The second, nature's rebirth, comes when the six-month dominance of darkness turns into six months dominated by light. And the idea of more than one start-date highlights an important traditional principle: there is always more than one way of looking at anything.

Following Chaucer's pilgrimage, this book starts its journey at the beginning of spring. But, in the spirit of more than one way of looking at things, it could have started at any time.[1] And you could always dip in and out as the year unfolds. Having said that, choosing to start now and finish at the end of winter takes us on a journey from the revealed and familiar to the veiled and mysterious. Of course, the months all blend together, each building on the last and preparing for the next, so whenever you begin it's a bit like coming into the cinema after the film has started. March–April's drama only becomes apparent when we recall what the world has just gone through, so a very brief acknowledgement of this month's backstory is in order.

Through the winter of 1846–7, in the northeast of America, Henry David Thoreau was in the woods, musing on time and nature. Alone in his cabin, he read Hindu scripture, which he thought could be from 'a previous state of existence' – did he mean an earlier *yuga*? – and which, by comparison, he said made 'our modern world and its literature seem puny and trivial' (*Walden*, 'The Pond in Winter'). Emboldened by his reading of the ancients, his observations of nature deepened. Venturing out as spring came and the snow and ice melted, he noticed that the patterns made by water running over sand anticipated the pattern of veins in the leaves that would soon follow. He wrote, 'No wonder that the earth expresses itself outwardly in leaves, it so labours with the idea inwardly. The atoms have already learned this law, and are pregnant by it' (*Walden*, 'Spring'). Thoreau saw that, even before leaves unfurled, the 'idea' of their veins was already 'in the air', in a way the ancient Greeks would have understood. His suggestion that spring's emerging leaves would outwardly express laws that their atoms had learned inwardly is a succinct and poetic crystallization of nature's activities through the winter months. (Here, they will be outlined in Chapters Ten, Eleven and Twelve.)

March–April's emergence from winter marks the end of a long and increasingly desolate period in which much life was hidden. Nature seemed in retreat, preserving her energies and waiting patiently in the hope of easier times. In Britain, for example, hedgehogs hibernated and the cuckoo, whose call once widely heralded the arrival of spring, flew to central Africa. Yet, as Thoreau suggested, winter in our thin, fragile biosphere was when forces from above and below – the heavens and the Underworld – were making ready for life's re-emergence.

IT USED TO BE SAID THAT MARCH can 'come in like a lion and go out like a lamb', a phrase that reflects a characteristic change in the weather, from fierce to mild. Yet – recalling Thoreau's 'pregnant' atoms – the phrase could also mirror the rigours of labour followed by the relief of childbirth, since this is when life on Earth seems to be reborn. Spring's arrival brings excitement and elation, but it also threatens sudden reversals of fortune as increasingly warm days are punctuated by sudden cold snaps. Each creature – and, as we shall see in Chapter Six, each dormant seed – picks its own time to emerge. But, while heaven's seasonal changes are slow and predictable, Earth's weather changes can be quick and unpredictable. So, every spring, some brave plants and animals are caught out and killed by frost. They are, in John Clare's words, 'by eager hopes undone' (*The Shepherd's Calendar*, 'March').

Each zodiac sign is ruled by a planet, and Aries is ruled by Mars. The month of March also takes its name from Mars, the god of war, so emerging life shows military urgency this month. Among the first leaves to appear are those of daffodils, whose veins do not show Thoreau's branched patterns but look more like the striations on a sturdy, sharp blade. Daffodils' leaves force their way out of bare earth like the spear tips of ancient Greek Spartoi, the mythical fully grown, fully armed soldiers who, according to Apollodorus, sprang up from strewn serpents' teeth (*Library*, III, 4). The advancing shoots are energetic, forceful, fearless and headstrong.

In his seventeenth-century *Herbal*, Nicholas Culpeper said daffodils were 'under the dominion of Mars', and Shakespeare noted that they 'come before the swallow dares' (*Winter's Tale*, IV, iv). Early spring's creatures exhibit Martial courage, being the vanguard who venture into the teeth of late frosts and show Martial discipline in their orderly sequence; daffodils before swallows, for example. And, after their daring entry, daffodils then open to show flamboyant trumpet-like structures associated with their male sex-organs. Now is a time of assertive announcements, and the zodiac associates those (humans) born under this sign with the phrase 'I am'.

Each sign is an expression of an element and Aries expresses fire, as the fiery Sun reawakens life in an apparently dead wintry world. Increasing light and heat prompt life to emerge, full of confidence, from the most apparently hostile of places, like the extraordinarily delicate soft white blossom that bursts through the blackthorn's tough, dry bark.[2] Leaves are the key sites that harness the Sun's life-giving fire, and the year's turn towards new life is reflected by the world's gradual greening, with innumerable leaves gracefully opening. Of course, on its own, the fire of Aries would dry out leaves, so it is tempered with water, or 'April showers'. This is an instance of the traditional principle that all things contain the seed of their opposite. As Shakespeare said, the 'Sweetest nut hath sourest rind' (*As You Like It*, III, ii). It is one reason why there is always another way of looking at anything.

WHILE MANY PLANTS and animals are killed by early spring's stop-start quality, some plants actually harness the unpredictable mix of sunshine and frost. All through winter, for example, the maple tree's tough buds were exposed to the elements. Those buds contained ingenious light-absorbing molecules called phytochromes which kept an eye on the weather and at some point – as days lengthened and light levels increased – they triggered the release of a hormone. Using the water that had slowly filled its veins when it started stirring through the late winter, the tree then carried that hormone to all the cells that engaged in storing food. Once there, the hormone triggered the production of an enzyme to break down starch; big, immobile molecules that the tree had squirrelled away last year ready to kick-start this year's growth. The enzyme turns every single starch molecule into thousands of much smaller sugar molecules, each of which dissolves in water to be taken wherever the tree needs food.

The maple's enzyme is amylase. We have amylase in our saliva and it works very quickly in our warm mouths, which is why starchy foods like potato crisps can taste sweet. In the cold early spring, maple's amylase works more slowly, but it still produces a steady stream of sugar, enriching the sap with a mobile source of energy. Over the next few weeks that sap will feed the buds, fuelling their initial growth spurts. After the buds have been given their first hit of sugar and start turning into leaves, photosynthesis will take over to make more sugar, directly harnessing the Sun's fire. This fresh crop of sugar will be used locally to feed more growth in leaves and branches. Whatever sugar is not needed there will be taken to replenish the stores, where it is converted into starch that, in twelve months' time, will be broken down again to kick-start next year's growth. The remaining sugar goes down to the roots to feed the subterranean fungi with which the tree lives.

Amylase turns immobile starch into mobile sugar, making many small molecules from one large molecule. According to the zodiac, this 'making many from one' is an expression of the divisive strife typical of fiery Mars, the god of war and this sign's ruler. (We are more familiar with fire's divisive qualities in the hearth, where a handful of logs is turned into countless millions of carbon dioxide molecules and soot particles.) Yet, since all things contain their opposite, this month's 'making many from one' is accompanied by some 'making one from many', an activity typical of Venus, the goddess of love. Venus' unifying influence shows in the fate of the rising sap, since many thousands of molecules of sugar will be bound together to construct one molecule of cellulose, from which the new leaves will be made. This construction of cellulose will increase as the year proceeds, but the deconstruction of starch is specific to the beginning of spring. Amylase's action is characteristic of a 'cardinal' zodiac sign, a sign that opens a season (see Glossary), starting activities that will be taken over by others. The

Venusian process continues – next month will be ruled by Venus – and becomes increasingly obvious with the greening of the world. On the other hand, this month's Martial breakdown of starch is completely hidden from view.

The making and transport of sugar may be hidden inside the maple but, in order to survive, creatures need to know what their neighbours are up to, and the tree offers clues about the sudden rush of energy at winter's end. For example, where their branches broke in winter storms, maples start to bleed and oozing sap seals their wounds, allowing the healing processes to begin. In March–April, through frosty nights, the exposed sap freezes, and something magical happens. The runny sap separates into a pure-water cap of ice above an ever-richer solution of sugar, like a freshwater iceberg floating above saltwater. The ice cap can be knocked off, melt or turn into mist and, when it goes, it re-exposes the now-stickier sap, which can freeze over again. The more often the sap freezes, the more water is lost and the thicker the syrup gets until all that's left on the tree bark is a sparkling crystalline crust of sugar. Coming across such a sweet tree-scab would be a godsend to a squirrel whose store of buried acorns was running low.

The maple grows in my own native England, but the frosts there are too mild for significant syrup production. However, in the lands that would, in time, be christened New England, Indigenous American communities watched and learned from the animals that feasted on the sugar that arrived just as their own winter supplies were dwindling. So, people started tapping the maple and, over time, they thickened the sap by boiling off the water, which was quicker than waiting for it to freeze off. According to Robin Wall Kimmerer, a plant scientist and enrolled member of the Citizen Potawatomi Nation, they responded to the tree's generous and sustaining spring-time gift by recognizing Maple as a revered leader of the Standing People (*Braiding Sweetgrass*).

MODERN PLANT BIOLOGY sees 'maple' one way, while an Indigenous culture can see 'Maple' another way. The American prophet of environmentalism, Aldo Leopold, said that learning to see one thing could mean 'going blind to another' (*A Sand County Almanac*, 'Clandeboye'). Yet, as Wall Kimmerer shows, that need not be true and, in any case, different points of view don't necessarily contradict each other. After all, the same landscape yields different vistas in different directions and from different vantage points. So, in this book's journey through the year, the views provided by modern science – like amylase breaking down starch – are complemented by mythic views from the traditional sciences.

Maple is significant for the Potawatomi. But, historically, their traditional sciences have had little or no recognized influence on how European understanding of nature or time developed.[3] So, most of this book's complementary vantage points come from the cultures that actually created the modern West's four seasons and twelve months. Today's calendar is a direct descendant of the zodiac, and the earthly vantage point that resonates most closely with the heavenly zodiac is alchemy, which was even known as 'lower astrology' because it treated the seven traditional metals as reflections of the seven traditional planets.[4] Of course, those planets play roles in the zodiac – Mars ruling Aries, for example – but fundamental to both the zodiac and alchemy are the four elements, commonly attributed to Aristotle (see Glossary). European alchemy developed from Middle Eastern alchemy, which had a greater focus on plants, also understood in terms of those same four elements. So, how might maple's – or, showing due respect, Maple's – timely gift look when viewed from the vantage points of alchemy and the four elements?

Maple's sugar appeared in Aries, which started with the spring equinox and which is the temporal bridge that leads from the dark half of the year to the light half. And the tree physically bridges two worlds. It straddles the dark, hidden world of roots and food stores, and the light, visible world of branches and buds. It brings riches up from the realm of darkness into the realm of light, and it does so around the seasons' bridge, since natural sugar production needs both the Sun and frost. For the starving squirrel, the tree's sugar arrived miraculously, like a glittering elixir of life. For early European settlers, it may have come via obscure processes that echoed the alchemical transmutation of lead into gold. After all, two of the previous three winter months had been ruled by Saturn, the planet alchemically associated with lead, while the Sun, which starts to dominate from this month onwards, is associated with gold. The English weather mirrors this transformation with 'golden' sunlight eventually breaking through after months of heavy, 'leaden' skies.

The engine that drives sugar's creation is photosynthesis, which, in alchemical terms, engages all four elements. It needs *fire* – in the form of sunlight – as well as *water* to join with the *air* – in the form of carbon dioxide – in the presence of *earth*, which is represented by magnesium at the heart of the chlorophyll molecule. (Magnesium is not one of the seven traditional metals, so it's not alchemically associated with any planet. It's found in rocks that fungi digest, dissolve and transport to the tree, which then carries it up to its buds and leaves. So, while the tree feeds the fungus with downward-flowing sugar, the fungus reciprocates, feeding the tree with upward-flowing minerals.) Saying that sugar is made from air and water, facilitated by earth and fire, is accurate from both traditional and modern scientific vantage points.

THE SUN'S FIRE-POWER has been enough to rouse nature from her winter slumber, but at the beginning of this month, at the equinox, day and night were the same length, so light and dark – or heat and cold – were equally matched. Days are now lengthening so the balance is shifting in favour of light and heat, but, throughout Aries, the Sun still has a fraction of the power it will have in Leo, for example, in the middle of summer. So, even after successfully navigating the danger of potentially fatal 'false springs', plants still need strategies for making the most of the available light.

Theophrastus, a friend of Aristotle, said the exotic tamarind tree opened its leaves through the day and closed them at night when it 'goes to sleep' (*Enquiry into Plants*, IV). And two millennia later, Carl Linnaeus proposed a garden clock based on when different flowers opened and closed (*Philosophia Botanica*). Closer to home and largely unnoticed, a humble plant that starts flowering this month also moves to a cosmic rhythm. The daisy – whose name is a contraction of 'day's eye', meaning the Sun – is regularly trodden underfoot, yet, as its name suggests, it keeps turning its face to the Sun through the day. The heliotrope, or turnsole, shares the daisy's affinity with the Sun, as its names in Greek and Middle English suggest. According to Ovid, the heliotrope was originally a nymph who was rejected by the Sun-god Apollo, the 'eye of the universe'. For nine days she sat sustained only by love, tears and dew, her gaze faithfully following the Sun. She then became rooted to the spot and turned into an earthbound, Sun-seeking plant (*Metamorphoses*, IV).

Ovid's account of the heliotrope's behaviour saw it as an earthly, passive response to the heavenly, active Sun. It took another one and a half millennia for people to start exploring exactly how plants could sensitively respond to the distant Sun. A key turning point was reached when, around the 1650s, the physician and alchemist Thomas Browne experimented by moving mustard seedlings around on his windowsill (*The Garden of Cyrus*). Nearly three hundred years later, auxin, a plant hormone involved in this phototropic, or light-seeking, behaviour, was eventually extracted from that age-old physician's diagnostic aid and alchemist's stock ingredient, human urine.[5]

Since all things contain the seed of their opposite – like fiery April's showers – so the 'rule' of plants' phototropism, or turning towards the light, has its 'exception' in skototropism, or turning towards the dark. Now, it might seem strange that plants which need the light should grow away from it, especially at the year's beginning when light is only just overcoming darkness. Yet climbing plants, for example, first need to find something to climb, so ivy looks for the shade cast by a tree before ascending. Only later does it turn towards the light. Ivy is skototropic when young, maybe starting its climb on the shady side of a tree trunk, and it matures into phototropism, perhaps flourishing on the trunk's sunny side.

OF COURSE, FINDING light is not the only challenge that plants face as the world reawakens. Fresh leaves are food for animals that have also just emerged from a hard winter. Some plants, like ivy, protect themselves from grazing with poison but, perhaps surprisingly, grazing actually stimulates growth in other plants, like some grasses. Now is the time when cattle come back on to the fields after having overwintered hidden in barns and, with luck, fresh grass arrives just in time for pregnant ewes that are getting close to full term.

Ewes can conceive in a cycle of about eighteen days, signalled to the ram by changes of oestrogen levels in their urine. Their pregnancy lasts about 150 days, so those lambs that are born in Aries will have been conceived in Scorpio, because the ram – which represents Aries in the zodiac – was naturally more inclined to rut in midautumn. The ram's urge to reproduce was heightened by changes in levels of a hormone, melatonin, which we share, and which, like the maple's phytochromes, keeps an eye on light levels. The ram is a traditionally Solar animal and it could be said that he was driven to create new life in mid-autumn because he sensed the days shrinking so knew that the Sun was dying.

Lambs could be seen to come from a heady cocktail of oestrogen and melatonin or, alternatively, the coming together of an eighteen-day earthly female cycle and a twelve-month heavenly male cycle. Either way, lambs provide one of springtime's most uplifting and heart-warming spectacles. Following the Sun's rhythm, lambs over-wintered hidden in their mothers' wombs and then emerged – like daring daffodils through bare earth – joyous and oblivious to life's perils.

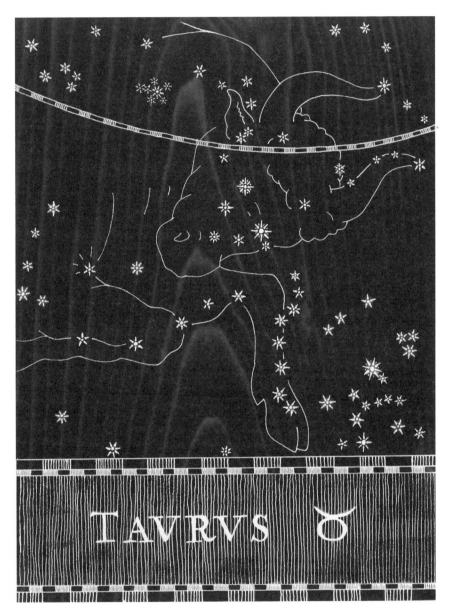

Taurus, based on star chart in Andreas Cellarius' *Harmonia Macrocosmica* (1661).

TWO

April–May
Fixed Earth, 'Flowering'

S chool children may have playground games like 'Pinch, punch, first of the month' but, as Thomas Mann said, adults have no 'fanfares at the start of a new month' (*The Magic Mountain*, v). Grown-ups don't celebrate because, of course, much carries on as before. In the natural world, from the start of one day to the next there is little obvious change, but from the start of one month to the next, the mood has altered. Last month had a shiver of excitement with its mix of novelty and jeopardy. Would new plants have enough stored energy to make the leaves that would feed them through summer? Would drifting snow threaten ewes and lambs with starvation and force shepherds to their rescue? Those perils have now largely passed.[1]

Last month's possibly faltering start has turned into a secure feeling that life has returned, that what had long been hoped for has now finally materialized. As the saying goes, 'April showers bring May flowers.' The sometimes-desperate striving after life has imperceptibly changed into the joyous possession of life. The zodiac associates those born under this sign with the phrase 'I have', and April–May is a time for enjoying the beauties that nature has brought forth. Carefree lambs frolic and gambol on rich emerald-green grass, with 'trembling tails' (John Clare, *The Shepherd's Calendar*, 'May'). The zodiac expresses this change in the quality of time with changes of constellation, element and ruler, and by moving from a cardinal to a fixed sign.

The constellation of Taurus is a bull, another horned herbivore, which suggests continuity with Aries' ram. Both creatures represent fertility and power, yet, in ancient ritual, only bulls were worthy protagonists and, even today, there are still bull-runs and bull-fights. Rams are just farmyard animals and are the lesser creature, so the zodiac implies an amplification upon moving into Taurus. If life was initiated in Aries, then it will be dug in and consolidated through Taurus. This month, life has found a sound footing and nature gains momentum.

Gaining momentum is reflected by the sign's element changing from last month's insubstantial fire to this month's substantial earth. The rate of change also seems to steady, like a sprint settling into a more sustainable pace, as befits a move from the most mobile of the four elements to the most stable one. The year also moves from fire's subtle influence to earth's dense influence, so that an elementally appropriate vertical ascent of life becomes a horizontal expansion of life. Of course, elemental earth is an ancient idea and not the same as the physical earth (which is strong enough to anchor huge trees while, providentially, being soft enough to be penetrated by roots and shoots). Soil is the humble, unassuming basis of life and it's easily overlooked because earth's activities are usually slow, unlike the dramas associated with fire.

As the second of spring's signs, Taurus is 'fixed' and is the second of earth's three appearances in the annual cycle. Elemental earth's first, cardinal appearance was after the winter solstice, in Capricorn, at the start of the calendar year. So, just as cardinal fire started the spring, cardinal earth started winter, and this month's fixed earth builds upon foundations that were laid down in winter. Earth is opaque, so winter's subterranean changes were concealed from view and it's only now that we are starting to see their effects as plants bring earth's hidden riches up into the visible realm.

In the zodiac, last month's ruler, Mars, has turned into this month's Venus. The year moves from the god of war to the goddess of love, and last month's raw muscular energy becomes this month's more refined seductive power. This change of ruler reinforces the elemental change because last month's fire was masculine while this month's earth is feminine. And since Taurus is an earth, or a feminine, sign, this month shows Venus' loving, receptive side (we will see her other side in the autumn, when she rules a masculine sign).

UNDER VENUS' REIGN at the very heart of spring, beauty seems everywhere. In May 1667 and 1669, Samuel Pepys recorded that his wife, Elizabeth, rose early to collect May dew, a precious commodity believed to confer a particularly attractive complexion (*The Diary*). Of course, nature's beauty is not restricted to April–May, and John Clare's poems, for example, evoke nature in constant circulation and can read like endless lists of one beauty after another. However, he lived much closer to the Earth than we do, and historic ideas about beauty and nature were quite different from modern ideas about beauty and nature. Nature's beauty did not only reside in picturesque landscapes or sunsets.

The modern saying 'Beauty is in the eye of the beholder' undermines beauty's traditional importance. Historically, there was a close relationship between Beauty, Truth and Goodness, the so-called Platonic triad (although Goodness might be better translated as Justice, as in just-right-ness). And, even before science and poetry got divorced, there were still many ideas of what constituted 'nature'. For example, in his *Georgics*, the Roman poet Virgil saw nature as the arena of agricultural labour, whereas in his *Eclogues*, nature was a dreamscape populated with humanized animals, plants and rocks, while in his *Aeneid*, nature's forces could be gods. There were also many ways of appreciating nature's beauty. For example, Virgil's near contemporary Cicero saw beauty in the fact that nature was orderly, nature was fit for purpose (or just-right) and natural things had unity and identity. Some of these links are still evident today in everyday words like 'cosmetic', which – like 'cosmic' – means ordered.

The beautiful order of nature was evident in the large and in the small, in the heavens' 'unvarying revolutions' and in the orderly sequence of life's annual emergence, like daffodils before swallows. The beauty of nature's fitness for purpose could be illustrated with Thoreau's branching pattern, which distributes water across a delta, and nutrients to all parts of a leaf. And the beauty of nature's unity or identity can be illustrated by any one of April–May's plants and animals.

JUST AS MUCH of Mars' raw energy was concealed – like starch being broken down inside maple trees, beyond the limits of our normal perception – likewise, much of Venus' seductive beauty is also unseen. Some of it is hidden in plain sight, with all her parts on show, but their coordination is beyond the limits of our normal attention. For example, to be fit for purpose – an integral requirement of traditional beauty – leaves must not only distribute sugar and minerals but also collect light for photosynthesis. One elegant way to maximize the collection of light is called phyllotaxis, with leaves spiralling round the stem to minimize the shade they cast on each other. These plant spirals are very orderly, for example circling a stem five times every eight leaves, and each plant has its own identifying rhythms. Yet all plants' possible spirals can be expressed with ratios of adjacent numbers (like five and eight, or ⅝) in the Fibonacci series – 1, 1, 2, 3, 5, 8, 13 and so on – where each number is the sum of the previous two. It is a widespread and extraordinarily graceful pattern of growth in nature, but its beauty is easily overlooked. Theophrastus noticed these plant spirals, Leonardo da Vinci tried to describe them mathematically, and they even engaged the attention of Alan Turing, the father of artificial intelligence. But, for millennia, plant spirals withheld their secrets.[2]

Some decades before Thoreau sat in the woods, Johann Wolfgang von Goethe sought to understand the natural world through the visible shapes that life-forms present to us, not through any mechanisms they might hide within themselves. His study of nature was guided by the study of art, and he took time to dwell in the sensual experience of engaging with nature while avoiding judgement. After much contemplation, he saw that all the individual types of plant in the world were just so many variations on one archetypal plant. He also saw that the changes that took place as plants grew were the different ways that nature could express the same archetypal idea (*Metamorphosis of Plants*). In this, he rigorously developed the insights of painters who – from ancient Egyptians to Paul Klee and beyond – have always seen parallels between the structures of whole trees and individual leaves.

From Goethe's vantage point, the fullest expression of a plant was its flower. Anatomically, many flowers are a nest of sepals that protect a whorl of petals that, in turn, advertise a cluster of sex organs. All these different parts are like modified leaves, following each other on a piece of stem that has shrunk so that the flower expands more in width than in length. Consequently, the difficult-to-appreciate helical spiralling phyllotaxis along a plant's stem is easier to see when expressed in the flower's single plane. The order in a flower arises from its symmetry, which is a way of seeing a diverse number of petals, and so on, as a coherent whole. Seeing the whole flower's beauty is a unifying experience that flows from Venus' influence of love, or 'making one (flower) from many (petals etc.)', the opposite of Mars' 'making many from one'. And, as specialized leaves, it is no surprise that the arrangement of petals and seeds in many flowers reflects the Fibonacci series. For example, different sun-seeking daisies radiate 13, 21, 34, 55 and 89 petals in delicate unity. Without even needing to count – because beauty is a mystery – it allows us to see 'a heaven in a wild flower' (William Blake, *Auguries of Innocence*).

IN HIS *The Descent of Man*, Charles Darwin acknowledged nature's 'taste for beauty' – like the peacock's flamboyant tail – but he and fellow naturalist Alfred Russel Wallace disagreed about why life should indulge in creating such beauties. Unlike the traditional sciences, modern science does not embrace the links between Beauty, Truth and Goodness, so nature's beauty poses problems for modern science. Darwin, for example, noticed that the overwhelming majority of plants had flowers and, in a letter to a friend, he described their incredible proliferation over deep time as an 'abominable mystery'. The goddess Venus, on the other hand, would encourage us to see the blooming of flowers as a beautiful mystery.

In the heavens, the planet – as opposed to goddess – Venus also displays a grand cosmic order yet, like phyllotaxis, her beautiful spiralling dance also goes largely unnoticed. Most of us only notice how a heavenly body like the Sun moves across the sky when we're sunbathing and have to shift occasionally to avoid encroaching shade. We might only actually pay attention to a heavenly body like the Moon if travelling off-road at night, going by full Moon if we want to see, or by new Moon if we don't want to be seen. (Every night on his 130-kilometre (80 mi.) trek home from the asylum, the poet John Clare lay down to sleep oriented with the Pole star.) Apart from these two 'luminaries', Taurus' ruler is the only planet bright enough to cast a shadow – on moonless nights – yet her stately dance across the sky is easily missed. As Venus' dance unfolds, the rhythm of her 'unvarying revolution' includes some repeated short reversals – as in some musical canons – which, for millennia, were appreciated by those who devoted quiet, extended attention to the night sky. For example, Plato noted that planets' general east–west passage was periodically interrupted by west–east movements, and he described their movement as akin to a 'spiral, rather like the winding coil of an acanthus' (*Timaeus* 39a). In Venus, this 'retrograde' motion occurs exactly five times every eight years.

Around the same time Goethe studied the beautiful order of plants and their flowers, the astronomer James Ferguson followed Venus' apparent motion for many years and plotted the planet's orbit as a flower with five petals (*Astronomy Explained upon Sir Isaac Newton's Principles*). His five-petalled mandala-like diagram was the result of dedicated meditation on a natural phenomenon, viewed through the lenses of both the old geocentric and the new heliocentric systems. (In the universe that gave us the zodiac, Venus went around the Earth in a perfect circle with circular 'epicycles' producing the retrograde motions. Alternatively, in Newton's universe, Venus simply went around the Sun in an ellipse.[3]) The seductive beauty of Venus' orbit, as seen from Earth, exists only in the mind of an inspired astronomer or traditional astrologer and is now known as the 'rose of Venus'. However, being emotionally engaged in, and moved by, that kind of veiled beauty is a sign that one is touched by a profound truth about nature. And the appreciation of such beauty is not idle self-indulgence. The pure, unconditional admiration of nature's mysterious beauty has been defended by many, including the great twentieth-century mathematician G. H. Hardy (*A Mathematician's Apology*). He followed the path of beauty in his quest for mathematical truths.

THE BEAUTY OF nature's orderliness escapes most of us because seeing it requires the sustained attention of a modern mathematician or the focused meditation of a traditional natural philosopher. Orderliness is easier to see in the predictable movement of heavenly bodies, but traditionally there are connections between planets and plants, as suggested by Plato's retrograde 'winding coil of an acanthus' and Ferguson's ⅝ 'rose of Venus'. And nature's beautiful order has always been appreciated by artists, like Hokusai and Van Gogh, who celebrated the brief but luxurious froth of delicate five-petalled cherry blossom that resides at the very heart of spring. Yet nature's beauties only come to those who – like Venus in her feminine mode – are open and receptive to the world. They included the early ecologist

Aldo Leopold, who saw a 'physics of beauty' as an integral part of his 'land ethic' ('Guacama' and 'Think Like a Mountain', *A Sand County Almanac*).

If order, fitness-for-purpose and unity all contribute to nature's beauty, then the order of phyllotaxis is fit for gathering light while the unity of a flower is fit for ensuring the plant's continued survival through time. The most beautiful flowers tend to be found on those plants whose reproductive process needs the help of others, so it makes perfect sense that flowers should seem beautiful to their insect partners. On the other hand, modern science can provide absolutely no reason why they should seem beautiful to us. After all, humans do not play any necessary role in plants' reproduction. Indeed, we have even created a toxic agriculture that is steadily killing the partners upon whom plants depend.[4] In fact, the flowers that humans find beautiful – those planted in gardens – are not all equally attractive to insects, which can visit some hundreds of times more than others.

Exactly what an insect finds beautiful is a mystery, but modern science can at least tell us what attracts them. Visual appeal is part of it, and insects sensitive to polarized and ultraviolet light could find apparently plain petals even more attractive because – hidden from us – they see patterns like landing strips and bull's eyes to guide them towards the nectar. Flowers' fragrances are just as important, attracting insects from a distance and again guiding them towards nectar. Yet, as those who mix perfumes know, the effect of any fragrance depends on its context, so different combinations in different circumstances have different effects. Whether seen as a Darwinian abomination or as a Venusian seduction, flowers' mysteries include the ways plants use their undeniably beautiful shapes, colours and fragrances to engage with animal partners and enhance their sex lives.

TO HUMANS, ORCHIDS are among those flowers that might seem the most overtly sexual – or, in the context of Venus, maybe we should say venereal – and their sexuality has been celebrated by artists like Georgia O'Keeffe and Judy Chicago. Yet paintings of flowers don't smell of flowers and, to an insect, the fragrance of a real flower can take sexual attraction to the next level. For example, Australian tongue orchids emit a smell that mimics the scent of a female wasp and is so powerful that male wasps can prefer the orchids to females. Male wasps can even break off copulation to visit an orchid where they attempt to have sex with the flower. In the act of trying to copulate with the orchid, the wasp ejaculates and picks up pollen, which it transfers to the next orchid that lures it in. Much wasp semen is lost in the process of pollinating orchids, and diverting males away from their mates might seem to threaten the wasps' reproductive cycle and their ultimate survival as a species. However, these wasps have solitary lifestyles and are genetically haplodiploid. (In haplodiploid reproduction unfertilized eggs become male and fertilized eggs become female. So, the more wasp sperm is spilled on orchids, the more eggs go unfertilized, and the more males are produced.) Being haplodiploid means that the wasp population regulates itself and the orchids get a plentiful supply of males to help spread their pollen.[5] However, in other cases, flowers that mimic fragrances can lure insects to their deaths.

A fatal attraction occurs in an extraordinarily strong and enduring keystone relationship between a particular flower and insect that is crucial to the survival of an entire ecosystem. Figs need wasps to pollinate their flowers, and wasps need figs to protect and feed the larvae that develop from eggs their mother lays inside the fig just before she dies. (The larvae hatch and dig their way out while their mother's body is slowly dissolved by enzymes inside the fig.) The fig offers protection to wasp larvae with a tough casing or synconium that surrounds its sugar-rich flowers. This mutually beneficial relationship has lasted for millions of years but is open to what might seem like abuse. It's perhaps not surprising that other types of wasp lay their eggs in figs without pollinating them, benefiting from the fig but not returning any benefit. Perhaps more surprisingly, some fig trees produce two types of synconium, only one of which will nurture the wasp's offspring. The type of synconium that does not support the wasp's offspring has the same attractive scent as the one that does support them, so it lures the wasp in to die, yet does not reward her death with life for her offspring. Nonetheless, these occasional deviations – exceptions to the rule that connects Beauty and Truth – have not undermined the extraordinarily resilient relationship between figs and wasps.[6]

These figs and wasps are not restricted to temperate zones with four distinct seasons – so are not specific to April–May – but they give a glimpse into the darker side of Venus that we will meet later in the year. After Aries' perils, life may seem securely established in Taurus, but the example of figs and wasps suggests that the life that has been secured this month is not the life of any particular individual, but the interconnected lives of whole species and ecosystems.

For the individual, some of springtime's beauties may have seemed to involve deception and exploitation. But since the ecosystems that possess those beauties are so stable and enduring, those exceptions seem to serve higher purposes, some of which remain a mystery. Unlike the impression created by jeopardy-driven TV nature documentaries with their emphasis on tooth-and-claw Martial conflict, ecologists are increasingly starting to understand life on Earth as being reliant on complex webs of mutual assistance and cooperation which, in terms of the zodiac, could be characterized as Venusian. Ecologists' studies of the natural world – like the coming together of a wasp and a fig to sustain an entire ecosystem – are starting to reveal the intricate beauty of dynamically balanced interdependencies, just as Ferguson's study of Venus revealed the beauty of its five-petalled eight-year cycle.

John Keats ended his *Ode on a Grecian Urn* with 'Beauty is truth, truth beauty – that is all/ Ye know on earth, and all ye need to know.'

This month's countless full and fresh natural beauties therefore offer a countless number of pathways to wisdom. Indeed, Ralph Waldo Emerson suggested that we should follow the bee's example by 'Seeing only what is fair/ Sipping only what is sweet' (*Humble Bee*).

Gemini, based on star chart in Andreas Cellarius' *Harmonia Macrocosmica* (1661).

THREE

May–June
Mutable Air, 'Mixing'

T he year's first sign was ruled by Mars and its second by Venus. As the god of war and goddess of love, Mars and Venus represent opposite sides of a reality that may seem divided. Yet, in mythology, together they had a daughter called Harmony (Apollodorus, *Library*), and in the zodiac it is as if, between them, the rulers of Aries and Taurus bore twins, Castor and Pollux. Following the ram and the bull, these twins represent the zodiac's third sign, and – like Mars and Venus – they are also fundamentally different, since one was mortal and the other immortal. Their mother was Leda and, according to some, they were born from a swan's egg along with twin sisters, Helen of Troy and Clytemnestra. The Gemini twins embody relationships, the often-invisible connections that link apparently divided realities.

Following Mars and Venus, Gemini's ruler is Mercury. The planet Mercury is fast moving and always near the horizon, between heaven and Earth, so its behaviour is appropriate to Mercury, the god, as the versatile and quick-witted messenger of the gods. (Mercury's mother was Maia, now one of the Seven Sisters, or Pleiades, who reside in last month's constellation, Taurus. The month of May is named after her.) The alchemical Mercury is both male and female, and Mercury's symbol is the only one to contain both a circle and a crescent, representing the influence of both the masculine Sun and feminine Moon. Non-binary Mercury embodies the fluid resonance between opposites, reinforcing the idea of an interconnected reality that is partly male and female, partly warlike and loving, partly mortal and immortal. Together, hermaphrodite Mercury and Gemini's immortal-and-mortal twins stand for a single reality of joined spirit and matter.

Elementally, Gemini is an air sign and, coming at the end of spring, this is air's final appearance in the annual cycle. Cardinal air first introduced autumn with changing winds, then fixed air found full expression in winter as the storehouse of information. Now 'mutable' air disseminates the qualities associated with spring, preparing for the next season, summer. Of course, dissemination is appropriate for a sign ruled by the messenger of the gods, and nature's messages – whether seen, smelled or heard – are all transmitted through the medium of air, this month's element. Yet air is not simply the passive carrier of messages connecting things in the world; it is also constantly created and re-created by the things it connects. For example, we breathe in the oxygen that was breathed out by trees, and the carbon dioxide we breathe out is, in turn, breathed in by trees. We share our breath with trees, or literally 'con-spire' with them, so the very stuff of air is the product of a natural conspiracy, albeit one quite different from the products of huddled, whispered human conspiracies.

JUST AS THE sound of voices is carried through the air, so too is the visible beauty of flowers. Bees – and butterflies, moths, bats and hummingbirds, as well as wasps and flies – all respond to flowers' messages, visiting them and getting covered with pollen, the capsules that contain a plant's genetic material. The flowers' visitors can transfer pollen from the male to female sex organs in a single flower or, to inject variety, between flowers on different plants. Pollen is protein-rich and, as well as delivering it, insects eat much of it, along with the flowers' energy-rich nectar.

Of course, we also enjoy the energy-rich nectar that bees distil. Four centuries before Christ, Aristotle thought that bees worked all year round, resting for only forty days after the winter solstice (*History of Animals*, IX). Writing within decades of Christ's death, Pliny said that honey 'comes from the air', like the 'saliva of the stars', although not 'before the rising of the Pleiades' and 'more copiously at full Moon'. He also knew about bees' division of labour, organization and discipline within the hive (*Natural History*, XI). Shakespeare identified the bees' different roles, including a 'king' rather than queen, as well as officers, magistrates, merchants and soldiers (*Henry v*, I, ii). Through the twentieth century, Karl von Frisch proposed that bees had a 'waggle dance' that told fellow foragers the direction and distance of flowers worth visiting. His studies inspired much research – note that 'in-spire' and 'con-spire' both play with ideas of transfer via air, or breath, respiration – but his work was also important for provoking controversies about the modern culture of scientific research. Not all scientists were willing to accept the evidence of other-than-human languages.[1]

The bees' dances may also include information encoded in sound. Their dances may contain meaningful sets of buzzes, and bumble bees certainly use buzzing to shake dry pollen off flowers' anthers. And messages carried by sound help other insects decide what to eat. For example, different wood-eating termites prefer different-sized pieces of wood. They decide what to eat by hitting the wood and judging its suitability from the wood's high- or low-pitched response.

Whether carried by sight or sound, messages come through the air and Shakespeare's Ariel – who embodied the spirit of air – sang, 'Where the bee sucks, there suck I' (*The Tempest*, v, i). The bee sucks big, heavy pollen grains from attractive flowers while the air sucks small, light pollen grains from flowers that are usually inconspicuous. This wind-blown pollen – mainly from grasses and trees – provides another side to plants' aerial messages because the other side of heavenly honey is potentially hellish hay fever. Last month we could be swept away by the beauty of airborne messages, but times change, and this month's vital airborne messages can cause discomfort. This month's sign acknowledges communications of all sorts.

SOCIAL ANIMALS LIKE bees, termites and ants also communicate with scents, or pheromones, that – as the wasp-luring orchid showed – can be mimicked by flowers. Humans generally do not perceive these fragrances, but they carry messages of life-or-death significance for insects, like raising alarms or attracting mates. For example, when male moths detect the scent of a female, they fly upwind until the scent disappears, then they zig-zag across the wind to find other pockets of air that contain the scent. Their complex flightpaths look strangely erratic to a casual observer but, by repeatedly finding then following a smell, they can meet up with a mate after being buffeted through several miles of turbulent air.

For us, ants provide the most visually obvious example of pheromones in action, as mixtures of ephemeral and enduring aromas that guide fellow foragers towards food and then back to the nest. These orderly lines of purposeful ants show how dynamic, distributed messages – 'follow me to find food' and more – can choreograph complex individual behaviours. Other scents even influenced how those individuals grew up. In ant and bee communities, for example, pheromones tell larvae whether or not to turn into a queen who will grow much bigger than the others, laying up to a million eggs over her lifetime. Other pheromones determine fertility within the nest, telling up to half a million individuals that the queen is laying eggs so they don't need to bother and can focus on other tasks. And when a queen decides that they should all move home, she releases other pheromones that calm the bees and keep them together in a swarm.

The diffusion of scent through the air is enough to coordinate relatively slow-moving bee swarms, but messages need to be carried much more quickly to manage more complex mass movements. Swarming birds, for example, mainly use sight to coordinate collective flights such as murmuration in starlings. Murmuration mainly happens through the cold winter and spring and is one of the most beautiful examples of swarming, with thousands of individuals moving as one. These vast, sinuous sky-dances create ever-flowing organic shapes, born from almost unbelievable synchronization. The flock has no leader and each bird flies in a manner guided by its seven nearest neighbours – those above and below, to the left and right, as well as those in front and behind. Harmonizing flight paths with neighbours creates order, and also smooths all local movements to allow changes in direction – wherever they may arise – to propagate gracefully through the whole flock. Yet some changes of direction are transmitted very abruptly – for example, when the flock decides to stop dancing, it can drop like a stone into its chosen roosting site – and no single bird can possibly see the whole flock. So, in addition to paying attention to the flights of its seven nearest neighbours, each individual bird probably also understands what the whole flock is doing by judging variations in lightness and darkness beyond its immediate neighbours. Darkness in a particular direction – caused by a dense mass of birds – indicates the flock's centre, while lightness, from patches of sky unobscured by fellow birds, indicates the flock's edge. Keeping an eye on a handful of neighbours against a shifting, blurred background of light and dark is enough for each bird to participate in, and co-create, something truly spectacular. Each individual starling has only a few quite simple options but, together, the flock creates extraordinarily rich dynamic structures. Flocks of starlings pulse, expand and contract, twist and turn, spin and circle, usually marking the time between day and night, as the Sun sets. And, unlike foraging bees, they will never dance the same way twice.

Today, starling murmuration has been studied as an example of how order can arise from complexity. Modern science appreciates starlings as natural 'information processing devices' that might inspire new computational strategies to be encoded in algorithms.[2] On the other hand, in the context of the zodiac and a Mercurial air sign, starlings demonstrate the amazing potential offered by a handful of very simple visual messages travelling through the medium of air.

OF COURSE, SHOALS of fish can show similar collective behaviours, communicating with each other through the denser medium of water. The zodiac cycles through all the four elements in turn and water's influence will be recognized next month. Yet, here in the changing Realm of Becoming, under the sphere of the Moon, all the elements are mixed together. So, while aerial messages are played out in the sky – where we might expect them – they are also played out beneath the earth. However, it is dark underground, so subterranean aerial messages, like those that connect and coordinate termites, usually do not involve sight but instead rely on the sense of smell.

When Henry Smeathman returned from Guinea in 1781 and reported to the Royal Society of London that termites could build towers taller than a man, very few believed him. In fact, the size of a termite nest can be hundreds of thousands of times bigger than an individual termite, surpassing human achievements. (In nineteenth-century Pennsylvania, the Reverend H. C. McCook calculated that the ancient Egyptian Great Pyramid weighed 69 million times more than a human, but an ant nest could weigh 6,800 million times more than an ant.) African fungus-farming termites, for instance, build massive nests consisting of 60-centimetre-thick (2-foot) cone-shaped defensive mud walls containing a well-protected underground royal chamber – barely bigger than the queen herself – beneath a strong baseplate. Above the queen's chamber is a central hive of nurseries, where the young are raised, surrounded by hanging gardens of fungi. The viability of such a colony depends on highly sophisticated air-conditioning systems that are controlled by complex air ducts that harness natural convection currents. Termite activity in the core of the building – growing and fermenting fungus – generates warm carbon dioxide that rises to an attic air-space and, from there, through air ducts into vertical ribs that project from the thick protective wall. The thin mud walls around these ribs allow the carbon dioxide to diffuse out of the nest and oxygen to diffuse in, acting like a giant lung. In the process, the oxygen-rich air is cooled and falls to the bottom of the building, around the royal chamber.

The construction and maintenance of the massive, complex and intensely dark nest are largely coordinated by smell. With the circulation of air being so important to the colony, it is not surprising that termites are extremely sensitive to air flow, and simple responses by individuals to draughts can involve plugging gaps in the walls that, if ignored, might allow intruders into the colony. Everywhere the air flows, it carries with it the Mercurial pheromones that also guide other behaviours. For example, when a termite rolls a pellet of mud, it transfers on to that pellet a minute quantity of a cementing pheromone. Wherever the termite leaves that pellet the smell endures for a while, encouraging other passing termites to also leave their pellets nearby. When enough pellets are left in the same place, the effect of the scent builds like a snowball and seemingly random heaps of mud start to become pillars. At a particular height, other airborne messages encourage termites to spread their pellets horizontally to make roofs.[3] Yet other messages encourage them to use other pellets to fill the spaces between pillars to make walls. Once the nest is built, a few similar messages also regulate the nest's internal climate by constantly redirecting the air flow – opening some ducts and closing others – to compensate for daily and seasonal changes of temperature outside the nest caused by the Sun's movement across the sky.[4] Different species build different structures with different ways of controlling their internal environments.

Responses to relatively simple airborne messages in ever-changing circumstances can cause very complex structures to emerge. In the case of starlings, those structures are ephemeral and made from the bodies of the birds themselves, but in the case of termites, the structures are enduring and made from cemented mud. The nests outlive those who build them, and the coordinated spoil heaps of other tunnelling termites alter local soil composition and change the eco-systems around them for up to 4,000 years.[5]

Studying the inner workings of termite mounds and tunnels is a very modern activity, and historic observers tended to focus on more accessible insect behaviours. For example, Aristotle and Darwin both noted that bees often visited flowers of the same type in sequence, sometimes bypassing other types. This might be good for the chosen flowers, but it is not necessarily the most efficient foraging strategy for the bee, and it suggests that insects don't mindlessly follow rules. Instead, they exercise choice. Individual ants, for instance, also exercise choice and judge the reliability of their memories, adjusting their behaviour to accommodate uncertainty. They can also draw on personal experience to modify socially sourced, pheromonal information. And individual bees also have personalities. In the hive, worker bees all perform a variety of different tasks, some of which involve lots of interaction with fellow workers while others can be carried out alone. It seems that individual bees can have preferences for relatively social or solitary tasks.[6]

NONETHELESS, MANY MODERN scientists seem unable to recognize the reality of animal intelligence. (At the same time, computers programmed with biologically inspired algorithms are instantly claimed to exhibit 'artificial intelligence'.) Modern scientists have two main problems with animal intelligence. One lies with René Descartes and the strange persistence of his belief that consciousness is only found within the confines of a human skull. Modern science therefore only very rarely grants intelligence to individual animals, let alone to collectives like starling murmurations, or termite or bee hives, or to the many dynamic relationships between different species, some of which we will encounter in later chapters. Another problem lies in scientists' relationship with teleology – the idea that all things happen for a reason and all actions are directed towards a goal. The premodern world, from before Aristotle to the seventeenth century, had no problem with teleology, and Pliny thought that bees' thinking was superior to human reasoning because, unlike us, they do no harm and always work for the common good. In the Bible, ants – like Emerson's bees – are 'wise' (Proverbs 6:6).

The zodiac associates people born under this sign with the phrase 'I think'. Approached with empathy, nature seems to think and, where we can see nature's actions fulfilling some function, nature could be thought of as an inventor or engineer, coming up with languages or building and running air-conditioned underground cities. On the other hand, where nature's actions are not so obviously utilitarian, like starlings swarming at sunset, perhaps nature could best be seen as thinking like an artist. Bees may dance to share information about flowers with fellow members of the hive, but starlings have different reasons for dancing. They seem to dance for joy – joined together as one – and the idea is reinforced by the historic spelling of joined as 'joyned', which might suggest they swarm simply because they en-joy it. Certainly, the standard modern explanations – confusing predators and so on – are unconvincing because starlings' very visible murmuration and deafening post-swarm roosting chatter both advertise their presence to predators extremely effectively.[7]

We might have difficulties in understanding how a starling, an ant, bee or termite might 'think', but, whether facilitated by sight or scent or sound, we know that their connections are all made through the medium of air. Historically, the mysteries of aerial connections were expressed mythically in the Language of the Birds – pre-Christian knowledge of which was won by dragon-slaying or, in the Franciscan tradition, by humility[8] – faint echoes of which survive in the idea that 'a little bird' might tell you a secret. While scientists might dismiss the mythical language of the birds, modern science itself is now uncovering even more mysterious aerial human– nature connections.

It has been recognized that merely being among trees promotes health, and being enveloped by the air that we share with such life-forms has measurable benefits. Just as flowers release insect-attracting scents, so it has been found that trees release molecules called phytoncides, which protect them from pathological bacteria and fungi and which, providentially, are also good for us. Breathing in the scents that pine, cedar and others breathe out has become known as 'forest bathing', and taking a walk in a forest has been shown to lower blood pressure, pulse rate, noradrenaline and cortisol levels, all of which suggest reduction in stress. Engaging in such a fragrant conspiracy with trees can also improve our immune response for up to a month and measurably increase our expression of anti-cancer proteins.[9]

Those health benefits are brought about by chemical messages that travel through the air, like the pheromones that guide insect behaviours. However, there are other health benefits that do not depend on the aerial transfer of material things like – admittedly, invisibly small – molecules. For example, it has been found that the view from a hospital window can influence rates of healing. The sight of a brick wall is associated with slow recovery while the sight of trees speeds recovery. Modern science has discovered that any contact with nature – like being caught in a storm, seeing a sunset, a tree through a hospital window, or even a dandelion pushing through tarmac – can induce feelings of awe. Awe is an overwhelming and be-wilder-ing sense of reverence, admiration or fear in the face of something that is greater than us. In traditional terms, awe is a response to glimpsing the Realm of Being that is normally veiled by the Realm of Becoming. In modern terms, awe is 'self-diminishing', placing us in a vaster reality and helping to put our problems in perspective. However you look at them, the feelings of awe that are inspired by the mere sight of nature have also been demonstrated to reduce stress and increase immune response.[10]

Together, androgynous Mercury and Gemini's twins represent not just the connections and relationships between male and female, love and war, or mortality and immortality; links between things that seem 'other'. They also represent the health-giving connections and relationships between culture and nature, whether nature is enjoyed in the wilderness, a suburban garden or a city park. Our connections with nature can be the scent of flowers and the sound of birdsong, carried through the air and taken in through our noses and ears. They can also be beautiful and awesome sights carried on rays of light through windows, to be taken in by our eyes. They are all messages of healing and belonging.

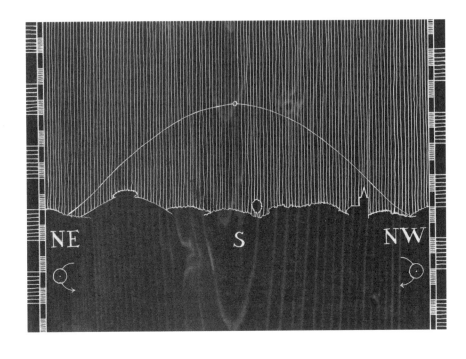

The Sun's path around the summer solstice at a latitude of 52 degrees north.

Summer Solstice

The word 'solstice' means 'when the Sun stands still'.[1] The summer solstice marks when the rising and setting Sun seems to stand still on its dawn-and-dusk north-bound journeys along the eastern and western horizons. Over a few days, around 21 June, the Sun's day-to-day movement slows, stops and then starts on its return, travelling back south along the horizons.

In England, the summer solstice is associated with Stonehenge. The whole complex took tens of millions of person hours to construct in three phases over thousands of years, and was the focus of pilgrimages for more than a hundred generations. In addition to connecting heaven and Earth, it also connected numerous diverse pastoralist communities and – being a work of wood, stone and earth – it ritually connected the living and the dead.[2]

Far from Salisbury Plain, in New York, the city's grid is oriented with the peninsula's coastline. By chance, Manhattan's northeasterly to southwesterly streets almost align with the direction of the summer solstice's setting Sun (and the winter solstice's rising Sun). The canyon-like streets point slightly south of the true solstice location, so they align with the Sun before and after the solstice, when northbound around 28 May and then again, when southbound, around 13 July. (Winter sunrise alignments occur around 5 December and 8 January.) Similar alignments occur in other cities. The continued cultural significance of such phenomena is suggested by the existence of a 'Manhattanhenge' wiki page.

Cancer, based on star chart in Andreas Cellarius' *Harmonia Macrocosmica* (1661).

FOUR

June–July
Cardinal Water, 'Nurturing'

C ancer starts with the summer solstice, when the Sun is at its height. But the Sun does not rule this sign. Instead, it is ruled by the Moon, and one reason becomes clear when we consider how the Sun and Moon dance together across the sky. The Moon's presence is greatest when it is full and – as the celestial mirror that reflects the Sun's light – the Moon is full when opposite the Sun. So, in the monthly cycle, the full Moon rises on the eastern horizon around the same time that the Sun sets on the western horizon. And, in the annual cycle, when the setting Sun has moved to its most northerly position on the western horizon, the rising full Moon moves to its most southerly position on the eastern horizon. Around the summer solstice, the daytime Sun is at its highest, and – maintaining the inversion associated with all mirrors – the night-time full Moon is at its lowest. This means that the full Moon seems closest to life on Earth in June–July. That is when the Moon is at its brightest, hugging the horizon, floating large and low in our earthbound eyelines, sharing its silvery presence with us on balmy summer evenings.

Although the Sun rules the twelve-month year, the Moon governs a thirteen-month year. In fact, the word 'calendar' comes from the Latin for 'to call', from the ancient Roman first sighting of the new Moon, in the manner still practised today in the Islamic world. The Moon also gives us the word 'month', the fundamental measure of time. The Babylonians knew the solar and lunar cycles were harmonized every nineteen years, and the number of teeth on the gearwheels of an encrusted mechanical computer discovered in a shipwreck off Antikythera suggests that the ancient Greeks had portable technologies to keep track of the cycle. Later, in the Christian tradition, the same metonic cycle became crucial to calculating the date of Easter, the movable feast.

This fourth month in the zodiac introduces the last of the four elements, water, which was the primordial element in many creation myths. For the Greek philosopher Thales, water was the source of all things. In the Christian tradition, God made heaven and Earth by dividing the upper and lower waters (Genesis 1:7). This month, cardinal water is in the midst of life, while later, autumn's Scorpio will plumb fixed water's inky depths and winter's Pisces rise to mutable water's giddy heights. Water is a feminine element and, together, the zodiac's three water signs could be said to reflect the three traditional stages of womanhood: the young girl (Pisces), the old crone (Scorpio) and now, in Cancer, the wife or mother. So, before the sixteenth- and seventeenth-century pioneers of modern science turned Nature into an unruly female whom they tried to forcibly control, philosophers and farmers could woo Nature as a virgin, partner her as a wife and respect her as a wise old woman. Starting from the spring, this is the first time we have met water and it is also the first time that water, as a cardinal sign, appears in the annual cycle. However, Cancer – as the time of the wife, mother, nurturer and enabler – is in the middle of life.

The sign is represented by Karkinus, the giant crab who came to the aid of a mythical water serpent but was killed by Hercules. Karkinus, or Cancer, was transported to the heavens in recognition of her loyalty. However, while the stars may have traced out the image of a crab for the ancients, their hieroglyph was not a stylized version of the constellation, like the zodiac's previous signs. Rather, it bears a strong resemblance to the Eastern *yin-yang* symbol laid on its side. As such, it echoes the upper waters over the lower waters, like the rainbow arching over Noah's round-bottomed ark (Genesis 9:13).

Again, Cancer represents the space between, as befits the crab, a creature of the shoreline that lives in the liminal zone between the land and sea.

Now, at the start of the new season of summer, Cancer taps into water's primal powers as the second of the year's transformative cardinal signs (cardinal fire started the spring). This month's ruler, the Moon, pulls water around the biosphere, that liminal shore-like realm between the heavens and the Underworld (which we will meet later in the year). And water's circulation starts the summer as the year's most productive season, building on spring's opening fire. This month brings an increase in the productivity that we saw in the previous sign, Gemini, whose twins reflected the conjunction of opposites in Mars and Venus, the rulers of Aries and Taurus. As the year unfolds, it is as if, this month, Gemini's twins have been handed over to the care of the zodiac's archetypal mother, to be fed and watered by the Moon.

THE WORLD'S WATERS respond most obviously to the Moon since the very highest high tides and very lowest low tides occur at every full Moon and new Moon. Maybe confusingly, these are called spring tides, not because they occur in the spring but because the sea seems to 'spring forth' to keep aligned with the Sun and Moon's dance every month. Appropriately, Shakespeare called the Moon the 'governess of the floods' (*A Midsummer Night's Dream*, ii, i). And the Moon not only governs the floods or tides, she also governs life within them. For example, the abundance of freshwater and marine plankton – whose name, like the word 'planet', comes from the Greek for 'wanderer' – varies with the Moon's phases. Plankton's surface population follows the Moon's rhythms because the fish that live in deep water come up to the shallows to eat plankton on dark nights around the new Moon, but they stay down in the depths around the bright full Moon for fear of being seen and eaten. Vertical migrations within lakes and oceans therefore follow the Moon's waxing and waning, with plankton populations declining around the dark new Moon, and recovering around the bright full Moon.[1] Other life events synchronized to the Moon include the mass spawning of corals, and this type of explosive breeding also occurs in some species of frog, while some birds, including nightjars, similarly coordinate nesting and hatching with the full Moon. Bats also coordinate their hunting activities with the Moon but – counter to modern vampire myths – they seem lunarphobic, becoming less active during the full Moon.[2]

Of course, the rhythms of bats and birds and insects, as well as of those mammals that feed on them, are now often disrupted by artificial lighting. And before our interaction with the natural world became industrialized, these lunar rhythms also guided human relationships with plants and animals, hence the extensive folklore of planting, harvesting and tree-felling at particular phases of the Moon. Sadly, most European versions of these folklores fell victim to the onslaught of twentieth-century science. As Annie Ernaux said, around the 1960s and '70s people just stopped talking about 'vegetables to be planted with the waxing moon' and started singing the praises of tinned vegetables (*The Years*). Yet now, late twentieth- and early twenty-first-century sciences have started to recognize the validity of equivalent folklores in other cultures.

For example, in the tropical Americas, palm fronds have long been used as roofing material, and it was commonly said that fronds gathered under a new Moon decayed much faster than those collected under a full Moon. Given that bat, bird and insect behaviours can vary through the lunar cycle, this Indigenous tradition made scientists wonder whether the variable durability of roof thatch might be linked to the palm's response to the creatures that wanted to eat its fronds. They discovered that the internal composition of palm fronds varied through the lunar cycle. Around full Moon, when insects were more active, the fronds contained more nitrogen compounds, which made them bitter and less palatable. They also contained more fibrous material, which made them more difficult to chew. It seems that the Indigenous harvesting and thatching practices recognized the palm's dynamic defence strategies and – by harvesting around the full Moon – they created a roofing material that was naturally resistant to insect attack.[3] So, early and mid-twentieth-century scientists' blanket dismissal of traditional European lunar animal and plant lore – without investigation – was obviously premature, and may well have been unwarranted.[4]

♋

LIKE HOMEMAKING HUMANS, bees also make 'cunningly wrought houses' (Virgil, *Georgics*, IV). And, although plants don't make special places for their child-rearing, their offspring do arrive at special times. In Taurus, under the goddess of love, plants advertised their sexual organs. In Gemini, under the messenger of the gods, they swapped their genetic information. Now in Cancer, overseen by the Moon, the consequences of pollen transfer start to show. Blossom petals have come and gone, long since scattered by the wind, plants' sexual organs have been transformed and, behind the withered protective sepals that remain, something is growing. The plant is with child. The apple blossom has become pregnant with a baby apple and it swells, like the waxing Moon that circles the heavens above. Shakespeare famously declared that 'All the world's a stage' and, in the next breath, acknowledged the tradition that human pregnancies and babies were both also governed by the Moon (*As You Like It*, II, vii).

Last month recognized the Mercurial connections that animals needed to make, in order to establish families and construct homes. With bees' and termites' complex custom-built nurseries there is obviously a question about whether homemaking or family-making came first, which poses unanswerable questions for the either/or binaries of modern science. On the other hand, the zodiac, with its traditional both/and spectra, embraces this type of chicken-and-egg paradox.

Whichever 'came first' in deep time, a home offers security for a family and, in birds for example, some form of nest-building usually precedes egg-laying.

Maternal care is so fundamental to life that it featured prominently in myth, including the belief that the 'kind life-rend'ring' pelican pierced her breast with her beak to feed her young on her own blood (*Hamlet*, IV, v). The myth of a self-sacrificing pelican crossed over into the Christian tradition and came to symbolize Christ's redeeming sacrifice. (We saw, in nature, that the mother wasp actually did sacrifice herself inside the fig, hoping it would protect and nurture her young.) The pelican also crossed over from myth to traditional science and, in alchemy, she gave her name to a tear-shaped glass vessel. The graduated tube at the top of this glass pelican bent over to pierce its round bulb, facilitating the repeated circulation of boiling liquids and condensing vapours. Such alchemical processes reflected nature's circulation of waters through the seasons, through the heavens and Underworld, and through our porous, liminal biosphere.

Maternal care was so important that even its apparent absence featured in myth. For example, the ostrich seemed to be an exception to the rule that birds build nests, and she was said to abandon her eggs 'in the dust', allegedly 'hardened against her young' (Job 39:14–16). Yet, of course, there is always more than one way of looking at anything, so it also came to be said that untended ostrich eggs were hatched directly by the heat of the Sun. This turned ostrich eggs into symbols of Virgin Birth and Resurrection.

$$\sigma_{\mathcal{Q}}$$

WHATEVER FORM IT TAKES, motherhood is life-changing, and maternal care is the expression of a profound, generative emotion, among the most deeply held feelings of which we are capable. The zodiac associates those born under this sign with the phrase 'I feel'. However, in the modern scientific laboratory, maternal care has been rebranded as a 'transgenerational epigenetic effect'. And carefully controlled experiments have revealed something that shepherds have known for millennia: that individual domestic sheep have different styles of maternal care, and, whatever their personal style – mixtures of protective, rejecting and laissez-faire behaviours – their mothering skills generally improve over time.

Care of lambs can be given by birth mothers and foster mothers and now, of course, also by humans, and we are not the only ones to tend the offspring of other species. Ants, for example, help raise the young of aphids and other insects that suck plants' rich, sugary sap. Aphids' sticky honeydew – which rains down from trees to cover parked cars – is actively milked by ants. In return for that sweet honeydew, they offer aphids protection from predators. When ants tend their herds of honeydew-producing insects, the number of nymphs that reach adulthood increases significantly and, while maternal care accounts for some of this increase, the ants also contribute to childcare. When no ants are present, the quality of maternal care can decline, suggesting that some mothers might invest more care in their young in part to ensure the ants' continued protection.[5]

Cross-species nurturing also occurred in myth. The god Saturn habitually swallowed his children at birth, so the next time his wife became pregnant she slipped away to give birth in secret (Apollodorus, *Library*). Her last son, Jupiter, was brought up hidden in a cave and nurtured by, among others, a swarm of bees. In recognition of the bees' kindness, Jupiter endowed upon them their very special nature, equipping them for difficult times that were to come. Although Shakespeare wrote of 'king' bees in 1599, bees are actually models of maternal care and, in 1609, vicar-beekeeper Charles Butler affirmed that the hive's sovereign was a queen (*The Feminine Monarchie*). For Butler, the queen bee evoked England's sometime-ruthless Virgin Queen, Elizabeth I, whose stable 44-year reign had just ended. Born poor, he had benefited from living in a country that thrived under Elizabeth's tight political control and targeted blood-letting.

Bees are haplodiploid – like the wasps that pollinated orchids – so unfertilized eggs become male while fertilized ones become female. In beehives, some of the fertilized larvae are raised in special cells and on a special diet of royal jelly, and those particular females become queens. (The other females are more closely related to each other than they would have been to their own offspring, had they become queen. Those worker bee super-sisters divide homemaking and child-rearing tasks among themselves cooperatively.) Queens reach sexual maturity after about three weeks and, between hatching and mating, a virgin queen will seek out and kill her rivals. On her nuptial flight, she will mate with a dozen or so males and store their sperm to be used as she sees fit, continually adjusting the hive's sex ratio. Through late spring and early summer, the queen is constantly tended by female workers who enable her to lay more than her own bodyweight of eggs every single day.

The queen can live around seven years and, when getting old, she may leave the hive with some of the workers to make a new home. But first they have to find somewhere to build it. When thousands of bees leave their old home, the queen calms them in a temporary cluster in a tree, while scouts look for new places to live and rear their young. The scouts return and tell the others – using waggle dances again – the locations of possible homes. These are collectively assessed and, when a quorum is achieved, they fly off together to the best location. When settled into a new home, the old queen may die a natural death or be killed after a new queen has established herself.[6]

In the second half of the nineteenth century, Sir John Lubbock, a friend and neighbour of Charles Darwin, put a beehive in his drawing room, left the windows open and made minute-to-minute records of each individual bee's activities. However, keeping track of them all was a significant challenge, so he eventually switched his attentions to less mobile social insects, getting ants to build their nests between two pieces of glass on a drawing-room table. Decades of study gave him profound insights into ants' behaviour and their perhaps surprising longevity. One of his queen ants lived over fifteen years (*Ants, Bees and Wasps*).

Bees helped delay the publication of Darwin's now-most-famous book because the popularity of beekeeping meant that details of bees' lives were – awkwardly, for him – common knowledge. The fact that an ordinary female could turn into an extraordinary queen simply by eating royal jelly was an embarrassment that didn't fit his theories. Darwin was biased by a focus on individuals rather than communities so, for him, the way a queen was made was a bit like saying a lamb could turn into a whale if it was fed plankton. He finally found a way round what he saw as a problem, but it has since been accepted that the realities of motherhood include many nuances, complexities and even contradictions.

♋

THE BIBLE suggested that ants gathered food and stored it for the winter. In fact, most don't bother, even if their visible rhythms might seem to suggest otherwise. However, in reality, the Bible was less interested in facts than in giving us examples or role models, and ants are definitely not 'sluggards' (Proverbs 6:8). Yet interpretations of nature and natural activities keep changing and, politically, the beehive turned from a theocratic paradise into a despotic nightmare. The males were downgraded, caricatured as stingless mating machines who were unable to feed themselves and forcibly evicted in the winter. In the eighteenth century, Bernard Mandeville turned the ancient images of a cooperative, socially interdependent organization into images of greed and selfish competition in corrupt, exploitative systems, driven by the relentless private pursuit of pleasure and productivity (*Fable of the Bees*). Beehives – and, for T. H. White, also ants' nests – became sinister models for the modern age of soulless military-industrial complexes (*The Book of Merlyn*, 7–9). The quintessentially Cancerian caring homemakers were turned into uncaring factory workers.

Mythically, the very real industry of today's bees is an echo of something we have lost. In the mythical Golden Age – also known as the Age of Saturn – honey was freely available to all and, thanks to Jupiter, bees' ability to distil honey from flowers is among the few remnants of that lost Golden Age. So now, in the later stages of the mythical Iron Age, the sweetness that was once a gift of heaven is more often won by relentless toil, far from the land of milk and honey.[7] Like self-fulfilling prophecies, the dark modern visions of bees have created an industrial agriculture that is now steadily exterminating them.

Campaigns to save pollinators endangered by habitat loss and pesticides tend to focus on bees rather than on wasps and flies or other equally important pollinators because of the bee's enduring potency as a maternal symbol. And its symbolic potency is brought about by its traditional image as a nurturing mother and its age-old association with the soul, our feminine aspect. Bees were said to anoint babies' lips with honey to produce 'golden tongued' poets and philosophers. The golden-tongued philosopher-poets included Plato and, if L. P. Jacks is to be believed, the poet-philosophers included a slightly less than golden-tongued late nineteenth-century breeder of spectacular Cotswold sheep ('Snarleychology II', *Mad Shepherds*). According to the traditional sciences, there's always more than one way of looking at anything, and for the poet Yeats, 'honey-bees' remained a corrective to human 'fantasies' and 'enmities' (*Meditations in Time of Civil War*, VI).

As the numerous different interpretations of ants' nests, beehives and queens suggest, the main cultural significance of natural phenomena is their potential to provide us with examples, role models or metaphors. And the Book of Nature is such a rich, multilevelled text that many diverse readings are possible, so, for example, Sir John Lubbock's reading of ants' nests, beehives and queens differed radically from T. H. White's. In addition to being a close observer of these sensitive and tenacious creatures, Lubbock was also a rich landowner and busy politician. As a landowner, he purchased farms around Avebury Circle and Silbury Hill in Wiltshire, southwestern England, and, as a politician, he introduced a Bill that eventually became an Act of Parliament. Those two actions – perhaps partly inspired by the selfless behaviour of the nurturing social insects with which he shared his drawing room – now ensure the protection of Britain's ancient sites, including Wiltshire's ancient sprawling monument to the eternal dance of the Sun and Moon.[8]

Leo, based on star chart in Andreas Cellarius' *Harmonia Macrocosmica* (1661).

FIVE

July–August
Fixed Fire, 'Ruling'

According to Aldo Leopold, there are two 'spiritual dangers' of being disconnected from the seasons. Those dangers are supposing that 'breakfast comes from the grocery' and 'heat comes from the furnace' (*A Sand County Almanac*). In July–August, we are least likely to fall prey to those spiritual dangers. Leo is a fire sign and, appropriately enough, it's ruled by the Sun. This is the year's hottest month and it comes a while after the solstice, when the Sun was at its highest, because the Earth always takes a while to respond to the heavens. Similarly, the coldest days of the year come about a month after the winter solstice.

This is fire's second appearance in the zodiac and it's the turn of fixed fire, with fire now enjoying its fullest expression at the heart of summer. Cardinal fire (Aries) started the spring, while, in a few months' time, mutable fire (Sagittarius) will end the autumn. It is as if fire lifted life out of the depths of winter and will prepare life to descend back into winter, while now it embodies the very opposite of winter. And fire's three appearances in the cycle of life echo the roles it played in Greek mythology, which had three major fire gods. For the Greeks, Hades, lord of the Underworld, was the god of fire's destructive aspect while Hephaestus, the divine metalworker, was the god of fire's creative aspect. Hestia, the goddess of the domestic hearth, personified fire's role as the preserver of life. In the zodiac, if cardinal fire seemed creative, while mutable fire will seem destructive, then this month's fixed fire represents the Hestia-like fire that helps maintain life, cooking food throughout the year and warming us through winter. Leopold's furnace borrowed and regulated the Sun's fiery power. It took the solar energy embodied in trees, either directly by burning wood or indirectly by burning ancient trees that the Underworld had transformed into gas, oil and coal.

Back at the end of spring, in the third sign, we represented Gemini's springtime vibrancy as reflecting a conjunction of opposites in the heavens – the union of the first two months' rulers, masculine Mars and feminine Venus. Now, in summertime, the expansion in earthly productivity could be seen to reflect an even greater heavenly conjunction of opposites, since the ruler of summer's first month was the feminine Moon and this month's ruler is the masculine Sun. But there is a significant cosmic difference between spring and summer. Spring was kicked off by the masculine ruler, Mars, who was followed by the feminine ruler, Venus, while summer was started by the feminine Moon, who is now followed by the masculine Sun. The importance of the feminine role was evident in nature with queens in beehives and ants' nests, so just how does this month's masculine sign follow in the footsteps of a queen?

THE PARTICULAR QUALITY of this masculine – so traditionally active – fire sign is suggested by the creature of the zodiac that represents Leo, a lion. The lion is widely known as the king of the beasts and is the head of a pride, a long-lasting, complex and flexible social unit that usually consists of more females than males. The pride's females are egalitarian and hunt together cooperatively, with each individual preferring a particular position in the hunting formation as well as favouring particular roles in the care and training of offspring.[1] The lionesses all have many moves – each one like the queen on a chess board – while the lion is like the king, a critical piece, but with much more limited moves.[2] The lion is commonly depicted as lazing around all day, basking in his own glory, while the lionesses go out hunting and do everything to maintain the pride.

Yet the lion's apparent lack of activity holds a key to the crucial authority, power and largesse that Leo represents in the zodiac. The previous four months have all been focused on activity – daffodils pushing up, blossom bursting out, insects exchanging pollen and mothers nurturing offspring – but activity needs to be balanced by rest. And rest is encouraged by the warmth of this hopefully most relaxing of months. Rest is even encouraged by the month's potential downside, which was acknowledged by the ancients as the inauspicious Dog Days that start when the sky's brightest star – the dog star, Sirius, in the constellation Canis Major – rises together with the Sun (*Iliad*, xxii, ii). Having these two heavenly bodies in the sky at the same time reinforces fieriness and traditionally brought the possibility of drought, fever and mad dogs.

Today, the ancient idea of Dog Days may still resonate with the British gardener, for whom August is a difficult month since all the early blooms have faded, the late blooms have yet to arrive, and flowers seem few and far between. Inauspiciously, garden birds also seem to disappear this month. (The word 'auspicious' is derived from the Latin for 'bird' and 'sighting', since ancient divination included the observation of bird behaviour.) In fact, the relative absence of garden birds this month is not inauspicious; they have finished breeding so stop singing and are moulting and consequently have become more vulnerable to predators. Sensibly, birds keep a low profile through the Dog Days.

However, many people who grow plants for food, not for display, can enjoy the Dog Days' positive side – leisure, possibly even enforced leisure – as they just wait around for their crops and fruit to ripen. And the birds that have disappeared from gardens may also have gone to enjoy the new abundance of food elsewhere.

Last month the apples on the trees were smaller than leaves and could still be more or less recognized as denuded, but developing, blossom. Under the Moon's influence the early apple still had an air of mystery, as a once-delicate flower's miraculously swelling ovary. Yet, as time unfolds from Cancer into Leo, the apples continue to swell and can now be bigger than leaves, looking less like parts of a tree and more like beings in their own right. Just as the Moon stirred the soul with strangely pregnant blossom, so the Sun now raises the spirit with fruit that generously invites us to pick and eat.

THE DISTENDED OVARY of long-gone blossom transforms into the mature ovary that is an apple simply by basking in Leo's steady fixed fire. The apple's maturing process involves the Sun powering the tree to create fruit sugars, and those hidden processes are signalled visibly by the fruit's skin slowly changing colour. The immature apple was green and, through Leo, it can become red. Or, at least, it can redden on the side that sees the Sun. In medieval symbolism the colour green can represent water – the element governed by last month's Moon – and the colour red can represent fire, the element that is fully manifest this month, under the Sun. In alchemy, reddening is a sign that a process is approaching completion, and the legendary Philosopher's Stone – as an elixir of life that transmuted metals into gold, the Sun's terrestrial reflection – was also, of course, red. Reddening is a sign of ripening, and ripening is the natural process of acquiring desirable qualities simply by being left undisturbed over time. Effortlessly ripening apples seem to just be there and, according to taste, ready for the taking.

In the modern world – with its globalized industrial food production – our feelings about nature's bountiful availability have spread far beyond the mid- to late summer orchard. Supermarket assumptions of instant availability now drive most agriculture, hunting and fishing, and as a result, humans have become the Earth's most dangerous predator. And, given the terrible ecological impact of our industrial style of food production, it is worth considering the behaviour of other top predators, which include – as well as the lion, king of the savannah – the alligator, king of the swamp; the shark, king of the seas; and the eagle, king of the skies. The previous chapter noted that queens in beehives and ants' nests have been used as political symbols. In the modern world, of course, the monarchies they represent have become unfashionable. Nonetheless, just as queens are fruitful metaphors, so too are kings, although sadly, the lion's domain has been so severely disturbed by human activity that it is no longer the most obvious creature to help us understand the role of nature's top predators. The apparent laziness of Leo's lion hints at an easy and relaxed relationship with the world and his seeming inactivity has a profoundly beneficial impact on his realm. That same easy-going relationship – and its positive impact – is more evident in the behaviours of other creatures that also live at the top of their particular ecosystems.

ONE WELL-STUDIED TOP predator is the shark-like killer whale or orca, another king of the sea. Orcas live in social pods – which are like lions' prides, except that each is led by a mother surrounded by her sons – and they prey on different creatures in different parts of the world. In the North Pacific, they used to eat the great whales that peacefully grazed on plankton. This sustainable predator–prey relationship held the populations of orcas and great whales in balance for countless aeons because the orca's appetite for great whales was very modest indeed, compared to human appetites. Humans treated the great whales that roamed the oceans as ripe for the picking, like apples in an orchard that enjoyed a perpetual midsummer. Through the nineteenth and twentieth centuries, the hunting of those great whales forced most species to the brink of extinction.

The collapse of North Pacific great whale populations in the 1950s and '60s forced orcas to change their time-honoured diets or starve. First, they turned their attention to harbour seals, which, though much smaller than great whales, were still relatively big, nutritious and easy to catch. But because the harbour seals were smaller than whales, the orcas needed to eat lots of them and, in the 1970s, their population started to crash. The orcas were then forced to turn to even smaller sea lions, which fought back but also steadily declined in numbers through the 1980s. Orcas next turned their attention to the even smaller sea otters – the killer-whale equivalent of an after-dinner mint – which led to another population collapse in the 1990s. The exact details of this ecological story have been questioned, but it successfully accounts for the sequential catastrophic decline in several marine mammal populations. Also, it suggests that human over-exploitation of a very small number of species (nine great whales) has changed the behaviour of a top predator (the orca) with far-reaching consequences. Those consequences have prompted numerous legal attempts to protect the North Pacific's marine environment. However, to date, all those protections have failed because the laws have been framed within a Darwinian focus on individual species rather than on relationships within mixed communities of many species.[3]

OF COURSE, THE consequences of humans over-hunting great whales have not stopped at endangering sea otters. In many places, sea otters had already effectively been wiped out – for their luxurious fur – by human activity in the late nineteenth century. Their removal from ecosystems has had further ramifications because the sea otters liked to eat sea urchins and, in the absence of their major predator, sea urchin numbers rocketed. In turn, sea urchins eat kelp, a type of seaweed, and, since there were no longer any otters to regulate their grazing, vast underwater kelp forests were decimated. They may be out of sight, but kelp forests are among the most productive ecosystems in the world and their destruction – directly by urchins and indirectly, via otters or orcas, by humans – is potentially disastrous. (In the context of the zodiac, it could be noted that the word 'disastrous' literally means 'ill-starred'.)

Even more hidden from view than submarine kelp forests are the swarms of micro-organisms and bacteria that live in them. They are grazed upon by the plankton, which are, in turn, eaten by vertically migrating fish. It has been calculated that the total weight of these micro-organisms exceeds the combined weight of all plankton and fish, and they are the basis of the food chains that support all marine life, including the last few remaining great whales and orcas.[4] It turns out that these marine bacteria are more than twice as abundant in healthy kelp forests as they are in areas of urchin-decimated forest, and their decline threatens widespread starvation.[5]

The consequences are not limited to the seas, because all the domains – savannah, swamp, sky and sea – of the top predators, like lions, alligators, eagles, sharks and orcas, are connected. One of the connections is provided by salmon. The salmon is king of all waters because it lives in both fresh and salt waters, and its cultural importance, as a wise Celtic king, survived into the twentieth century, punningly hidden in and leaping through Joyce's *Finnegans Wake*. Salmon spend a few months or years in the streams where they were born, then migrate to the open sea, where they continue to grow before returning to fresh water to spawn and, usually, die. In their whole lives they can roam many thousands of kilometres, and their final journey – often to the place where they were born, guided by a memory of its particular smell – can involve a climb of up to 2,000 metres (1.2 mi.). Yet they might not be able to complete the circle and die where they were born. On their way home they might be caught and eaten by a bear. Salmon can weigh many kilograms and they put on most of their weight while living in the ocean, so the carcass of an old, returning salmon contains much nutritious nitrogen that comes from the sea. That nitrogen in the salmon's flesh ends up fertilizing the soil that surrounds the stream where it was caught and eaten, excreted either in the bear's urine or by those who scavenge the bear's leftovers. Fungi then transport the nitrogen from the soil to neighbouring plants. Ecological isotope studies show that, within half a kilometre (0.3 mi.) of salmon-spawning streams, between a sixth and a quarter of all the nitrogen in (spruce) trees comes from the ocean.[6]

The positive influences of those at the top of food chains – like bears and salmon – on the bottom of the food chain – like scavengers and spruce – are now known as 'trophic cascades' and their disruption by the killing of top predators is recognized as a major cause of ecological collapse.[7] Although he did not use the phrase, the idea first appeared in Leopold's writings when he reported looking into the dying eyes of a wolf he had shot. He saw that, by preying upon deer, the wolf had saved the mountain from overgrazing and erosion. Without a wolf to protect it, the mountain – its trees decimated, and its soil no longer bound by roots – would, piece by piece, make its way to the sea, slowly silting up and choking rivers on its way. Leopold realized that 'a mountain lives in mortal fear of its deer', just as deer lived in fear of the wolf (*A Sand County Almanac*).

FEAR OF TOP predators is age-old but, historically, it has also been mixed with respect and compassion. For example, the Irish St Maedoc of Ferns repeatedly fed hungry wolves, echoing St Antony of Egypt and St Luke and their relationships with their local top predator, the lion. Again in Ireland, an otter brought salmon to feed St Coemgen through Lent and, on his sea voyages, the nomadic St Brendan repeatedly celebrated Easter on the back of an obliging whale, while his island paradise abounded with salmon (*Bethada Náem nÉrenn*). Irish saints' relationships with salmon reflect the salmon king's association with wisdom in Celtic mythology. Hints of an even older understanding of the critical link between the very top and bottom of the food chain can be seen in the cultural practice of sacrificing the king – upon the failure of a harvest – to revive Mother Earth's fertility. Mythically, this echoes the way that salmon naturally sacrifice themselves to the soil that surrounds their birthplace.

The lion's apparent inactivity is therefore not indolence, but a regal model of ease, moderation and benevolence. In the zodiac, the sign of Leo is known as the Golden Child, the empowered self that emerges from the union of fire and water or the union of the Sun, king of the day, and the Moon, queen of the night. The Golden Child, like the golden apple, manifests the next generation. (Interestingly, the word 'generation' once referred to a process, but now usually refers to a product.[8]) The zodiac associates those born under this sign with the phrase 'I will'. And, as the zodiac's position of power, it is also the position where choice can be exercised. Following the lion's example, 'I will' could equally be 'I will not'. At the food chain's apex, the lion has permission to do as he pleases, and the ideas of permission and pleasure are related to licence and leisure. This leisurely month offers the chance to contemplate and decide, so the lion's licence to kill is equally the licence to not kill. In fact, much of the behaviour of creatures further down the food chain is regulated by fear of a ruler that, more often than not, actually causes little harm – hence the long-sustained premodern relationship between the North Pacific's orcas and great whales. The human failure to emulate that relationship is a serious perversion of the natural order.

THE LEISURE, AND THE LICENCE, of Leo's king of the beasts has become politically unfashionable – like the queen's control of her hive – because the recent industrialized past encourages us to associate leisure with money and privilege. Yet all levels of society in the pre-industrial world generally enjoyed more leisure than we do today. This is evident from the number of our secular holidays compared with the premodern calendar's many holy days. Workers in medieval Europe were expected not to be productively engaged in their trades on anywhere from forty to sixty local saints' days, plus the whole weeks of Christmas, Easter and Whitsun as well as 52 Sabbaths.

Leisure comes when we are not disturbed by immediate needs, and it permits desirable qualities to arise within us, just as the apple acquires desirable qualities upon ripening, when left undisturbed under Leo's Sun. And one of the desirable qualities that can arise in us is an interest in the wider world which, according to Plato, comes 'only when communities have leisure' (*Critias*, 11). It is therefore not surprising that Irish saints, who lived without haste or distraction, were able to establish profoundly trusting relationships with the animals among which they lived. Nor is it surprising that, centuries later, it was a leisurely country curate, the Reverend Gilbert White, who was able to divine the auspicious unfolding of seasons by observing the order of visiting birds – first swallows, then martins, then swifts – birds that, to a busy modern person, can be hard to even distinguish, let alone sequence.[9]

Similarly, Sir John Lubbock was the son of a bank director who enjoyed much more leisure than late nineteenth-century industrial mill-workers. In addition to spending his leisure time observing ants, he even tried to teach his pet poodle to read with one of his daughters. And in his role as a politician, as well as saving Avebury Circle and Silbury Hill, he also – aware of the leisure afforded by his privileged background – drafted the 1871 Bank Holiday Bill, creating the first secular holidays in British history.[10] In his honour, the first one was popularly known as St Lubbock's day.

In July and August, the weather encourages leisure. But, while the days are hot, they are also getting shorter. The Sun's decline had been slow through June–July but it speeds up through July–August. Gradually, the seasonal shortening of day-length can no longer be hidden behind the daily variations of cloud cover at dawn or dusk. By the end of Leo, a period of repose, we start to sense that change is just over the horizon.

Virgo, based on star chart in Andreas Cellarius' *Harmonia Macrocosmica* (1661).

SIX

August–September
Mutable Earth, 'Serving'

Following life's explosive start under Aries and its gradually slowing pace, any activity at all could be difficult through the Dog Days, with the now-parched grass's emerald-green glitter a distant springtime memory. Now, in Virgo, the last month of summer, it is as if the finishing line is in sight and we can see the light at the end of the tunnel. Actually, that phrase betrays our cultural bias towards the light – as opposed to the dark – when, strangely, the relief from baking August days comes with nightfall and darkness. Yet perhaps our cultural bias is not too surprising. After all, we see plants' stems and leaves seeking light, but we don't see their roots' opposite yet equally necessary dark-seeking behaviours.

This month, those apples that remain on the tree weigh down its bending boughs and we can imagine the desire of these solid spheres to return to earth, the solid sphere from which the tree itself sprang many years ago. The tree needed light and air to fuel its growth and spread its pollen, and the apple needed light and air to swell and sweeten. And springtime's delicate blossom looked completely at home in the air, yet, now, late summer's heavy apples look quite precarious, and maybe even slightly incongruous, up in the air. If not picked soon they will fall, and their precious cargo of seeds will return to earth.

Modern mythology tells us that one particular apple's fall to earth was interrupted when it hit Isaac Newton's head. The story is not true, but it has stuck in the imagination because the clash of two spheres – an apple and a skull – resonates with Newton's cradle and his theory that gravity is a force that acts between two masses. However, before Newton, the falling apple was not seen as the powerless victim of some grand impersonal force. Traditionally, it was seen as an independent agent that made a choice. At some point, the apple decided that it had accumulated sufficient food reserves – enough to persuade a creature to eat it and distribute its seeds – so nutrients stopped flowing through its stalk and it let go of the tree. It journeyed through the air, from a laden tree-bough to the bounteous earth, just as a bubble journeys – in the opposite direction – through the water, from a muddy pond-bottom to the expansive sky. According to traditional science, the apple and bubble's voyages are both cases of 'like seeking like': a small solid sphere seeking a vast solid sphere, and a small gaseous sphere seeking a vast gaseous sphere. To move, the airborne apple harnessed its inherent gravity, and the water-borne bubble its inherent levity, but both were homeward bound.

Apple trees surround their relatively unpalatable seeds with something good to eat, but other seeds can be good to eat in their own right. For instance, grasses put most of their energy into their seeds as part of a strategy of growing fast and lean, instead of slowly building enduring structures like trees. Around 10,000 years ago people took advantage of grasses by selectively breeding them, domesticating three key cereals: maize in Meso-America, rice in China and wheat in the Middle East. Today, the seeds from just these three plants provide about half of the total energy needs for all humans across the globe. Seeds ensure the cycle of life on Earth continues by fuelling many creatures but also, one way or another, by going underground and ensuring next year's crop.

VIRGO IS THE zodiac's mutable earth sign and August–September is when the summer's accumulated riches are distributed. Leo ended with a feeling of change around the corner and Virgo prepares for that change. The sign is ruled by the planet Mercury and, since this is the second time Mercury has appeared in the year (the first time was in Gemini), this is perhaps the place to acknowledge the pattern of the zodiac's ruling planets. The last two months were ruled by the Moon and Sun, and – in the traditional zodiac – the other ten months are ruled by the five remaining planets, each ruling twice and in the same order as their nested orbits in the premodern cosmos. In the geocentric universe, the orbits of these five ruling planets – Mercury (close to Earth), Venus, Mars, Jupiter and Saturn (close to the fixed stars) – are like the rungs of a cosmic ladder. Starting the year in Aries, we were on the way down that cosmic ladder, going from Mars to Earth's closest neighbour, the Moon. But, for the next five months, we will go up that ladder, from Mercury in Virgo all the way to Saturn in Capricorn. We first met Mercury coming down the ladder and now we meet it again on the return journey, as if heavenly influences were coming down to Earth in the year's first half, and now, approaching the year's second half, those influences are leading back to heaven. Having established the material side of life, this month prepares the ground for the spiritual side of life's journey.

Mercury the messenger first appeared in Gemini, the mutable expression of subtle air, and now Mercury is in Virgo, the mutable expression of dense earth. Back in airy late spring, Mercury oversaw the transfer and exchange of ephemeral sights, sounds and scents or almost weightless grains of pollen. Now, in earthy late summer, Mercury oversees the transfer and exchange of substantial and heavy things, like full-grown apples that need to assess when would be the best time to part company with the tree and go back to earth. In addition to being the messenger of the gods, Mercury was also the patron of scientists and artists, of merchants and thieves, of people who exchange ideas or goods and assess risks and benefits. The zodiac associates those born under this sign with the phrase 'I analyse'.

In 1678 Andrew Marvell recognized that the 'industrious bee/ Computes its time as well as we' in order to coordinate with flowers that open and close through the day, as in Linnaeus' garden clock. Exactly how the bee 'computed' the time and how the flowers analysed, or 'reckon'd', the 'hours' is largely hidden from us (*The Garden*). And over the next six months, nature and her modes of analysis will become even more hidden. Under Mercury's airy influence, we saw that termites worked out how to construct air-conditioned cities and starlings worked out how to coordinate hypnotic collective flight paths. But under Mercury's earthy influence, nature's analysis is harder to see. For example, plant seeds – which, unlike insects' or birds' eggs, may appear to have been deserted by their parents – have, in fact, been fully equipped to sense and respond to the unseen maternal care offered by earth. Like the daring daffodil bulb, even the smallest apparently dried-out seed that lies underground is able to assess its life-chances and decide when to germinate. It analyses its immediate circumstances and the problems they pose or the opportunities they offer.

Buried seeds need to time their germination so that they have a good chance of meeting favourable circumstances when they eventually emerge. As vulnerable saplings, they will need space above ground as well as light, water and enough warmth to sustain young growth. In other words, seeds need to predict the future. This is easier in temperate zones with four seasons than in more hostile and less predictable climate zones. For example, after tens of millions of years of experience, many Australian plant seeds have learned how to predict their best chances of survival in environments that are periodically ravaged by fire. When dormant, literally 'sleeping', these seeds are aware of the soil's average temperature, so they know when they are in relatively hot or cold seasons. They also keep track of the soil's moisture content, possibly over many years, so they know when they are in relatively wet or dry seasons. However, while temperature and moisture levels fluctuate in more or less regular seasonal cycles, destructive fires – bushfires that clear undergrowth, and fiercer wildfires that also clear mature standing trees – are much less predictable.

Buried dormant seeds are aware of what goes on immediately overhead because they are also sensitive to brief, rapid increases in soil temperature, hot for bushfires and even hotter for wildfires. Seeds continuously monitor the fast changes to higher temperatures as well as slow changes in temperature and moisture, and the right combination of changes will awaken them from dormancy. The smoke and soot particles that percolate down into the soil after a fire also play a vital role for the awakening seeds. This is because smoke contains partially burnt plant matter, including molecules called karrikins, which are similar to hormones found around established plants' roots. The smoke's hormone-mimicking karrikins encourage the growth of fungi in the soil, and these will become the seed's much-needed companions after it germinates. (We will meet plants' subterranean fungal companions in the next mutable sign, Sagittarius.) So, smoke acts as a trigger to those who already live around the sleeping seed, and they respond by getting ready to feed the seedling immediately after it awakens.[1]

Bushfires and wildfires also clear space above ground so, after a fire, seedlings and saplings can be sure of light, even though they might face competition from other newly awakened young plants. So, to increase their life-chances, different seeds germinate after different sequences and combinations of change in temperature and moisture and fire or smoke. And parent plants can also hedge their bets by producing heteromorphic seeds with characteristics that are identical in all respects except for these dormancy-breaking combinations and thresholds. Seemingly sleeping seeds' real-time monitoring of, and response to, constantly changing soil conditions has ensured the survival of thousands of species for millions of years. Yet such plants also have their own time thresholds. To survive they need a minimum of fifteen to fifty years between conflagrations, so they are now threatened by climate change and the increased frequency of forest fires.[2]

ANY THREAT TO plants is, of course, also a threat to the animals that live with them – either above the earth or buried within it – and those lives can also have critical time thresholds. For example, some types of North American cicada emerge together from the soil once every thirteen or seventeen years. Their almost magical, spectacularly synchronized appearance has earned them the name *Magicicada* from the usually unpoetic scientific community. Their cycle of appearances in our world – like a plague of locusts, over a couple of months from late spring to summer – occurs like clockwork. Around this month, after such a mass appearance, the next generation of cicadas are starting their lives in the Underworld, in egg, then larval stages, unseen, in the soil and living off the sugary sap they suck from tree roots, like heavy subterranean versions of the aphids that are herded and milked by ants.

The numbers thirteen and seventeen are prime numbers, meaning they cannot be divided by any other number than one or themselves. As a result, the *Magicicada*'s above-ground appearances will not consistently coincide with the appearances of other types of cicadas that emerge above ground in cycles of every two, three or more years. They therefore rarely meet – or breed with – any other types of cicada, and, over millennia, this may have set them apart as a breed.[3] No one knows how they coordinate their emergence. Perhaps they monitor the annual rhythms of sap flow in tree roots, as rutting rams monitor the lengthening of autumnal nights. What is clear, however, is that nature has mysterious ways of coordinating extraordinarily complex patterns of behaviour, even in subterranean grubs and sleeping seeds.

The cicadas' life cycles were known by those who shared the land with them, and, for the ancient Greeks, they were autochthonic, or born from the Earth, embodying the spirit or the genius of the land. In 1633, after one mass appearance of New England's *Magicicada*, Governor William Bradford reported that the Indigenous community warned settlers that sickness would follow, as indeed it did (*Of Plymouth Plantation, 1620–47*). The Indigenous community's foreknowledge may have drawn upon the First Beings' Original Instructions, which included reverence for the four elements. On the other hand, the seventeenth-century settlers may have interpreted their neighbours' uncanny prediction in terms of the zodiac. Modern science tries to understand cicadas' rhythms – and some consequences of their swarming – in terms of genetics and mathematics. Different cultures have different ways of analysing the same phenomenon.

IN THE SEVENTEENTH century, female natural philosophers, such as Margaret Cavendish, were rare, and only grudgingly tolerated. European science became an almost exclusively male pursuit and it started studying nature by, paradoxically, retreating from nature. Scientists withdrew from the messy, complicated outside world and moved into the orderly, constructed space of the laboratory, where they attempted to control specially selected aspects of nature. Modern science's analysis mainly continues this legacy of isolating bits of nature and treating natural phenomena as unruly and in need of control. Yet the traditional ways of analysing nature – with engagement and sympathy – did not completely disappear. For example, the nineteenth-century son of a Wiltshire farmer, Richard Jefferies, wrote that 'so ready are all creatures to acknowledge [human] kindness' that he could count among his friends a swarm of wasps ('His Dominions', *The Game Keeper at Home*). Around the same time, as a landed country gentleman, Charles Darwin also had some sympathy with the animals he studied. In fact, Darwin's greatest contribution to the science of life may have been his gradual development – and his prolonged demonstration – of a completely new emotional way in which humans could interact with other life-forms.

Like his friend and neighbour Sir John Lubbock, Darwin kept all his observations about animals in numerous diaries, some of which he stored locked away in private safe spaces, like the controlled laboratories into which the experimental scientists had retreated. Some of these diaries contained the seeds of his ideas and they downplayed personal issues, in keeping with the Protestant tradition of documenting the soul's journey. These particular diaries were examples of spiritual accounting, of self-discipline, of purification and a reckoning with God via His creation. Yet Darwin also kept other diaries – the ones in which he worked up his ideas for public consumption – and they had a completely different tone. Paradoxically, these passionately aspired to cool objectivity, seemingly driven by a fearful dread of falling into the perceived dangers of subjectivity. These two very different types of diary show that Darwin was a divided man. He was someone who could happily dissect a pinned-down bird while his pet dog lay curled up at his feet. He knew that emotion was a vital way of connecting with others – including dead birds and living dogs – but he reduced emotion to measurable quantities, like heart rates and blood pressures. He substituted data for feelings in order to assemble many apparently disconnected details – particular case studies – into a grand narrative. This emotionally divided self was the price that he paid for his grandest narrative, the theory of evolution.[4]

Darwin's now-most famous book was the result of an epic and sometimes gruelling five-year voyage to the other side of the world. Yet the book he wrote that was most popular in his lifetime was the result of a casual conversation in his uncle's backyard. Darwin's uncle pointed out some bricks, casually discarded some years earlier, that were now under inches of soil. His uncle suspected that they had been buried by earthworms and Darwin pursued this hunch. (In fact, Gilbert White had suggested that the study of earthworms could 'afford much entertainment and information' about a century earlier.[5]) After decades of study, Darwin calculated that there were more than 50,000 earthworms per acre and that, between them, they moved 18 tons of soil per year. Over a century later, modern research suggests that both numbers were serious underestimates, and the modest earthworm has now been recognized as a vital ecosystem engineer.

Working all year round, earthworms' activities are not specific to this month but, by constantly recycling topsoil, they are obviously agents of this zodiac sign's mutable earth. Perhaps surprisingly, they also manifest Virgo's analytical trait.

Darwin assessed earthworms' powers of perception. He thought they were practically blind and was convinced they were deaf, since they didn't respond when his son serenaded them with his bassoon. He considered earthworms to be mainly tactile but nonetheless thought they had significant 'mental powers' (*The Formation of Vegetable Mould*). Darwin observed earthworm behaviours and concluded that, despite their limited senses, they exhibited intelligence.

In modern science, intelligence has been contrasted with instinct, just as learned or acquired behaviour is contrasted with innate or in-herited behaviour, and nurture with nature. While valid, these modern distinctions can be quite artificial and can create chicken-and-egg problems that are merely side-effects of a particular chosen vantage point. Darwin himself shied away from those distinctions and merely observed behaviours, not worrying whether or not they might be 'intel-ligent' or 'instinctual'. He preferred to simply consider whether or not they were appropriate to circumstances. He decided that one aspect of earthworm behaviour – pulling leaves into their burrows – was indeed appropriate to circumstances. He guessed that it was intended to stop cold air entering their burrows, since they didn't bother to seal their wormholes with leaves when living in pots in his nice warm drawing room. By systematic experimentation, he found they preferred leaves that would most efficiently line their burrows and saw that they pulled them by the part of the leaf that would most easily enter the burrow. From all this, he inferred that earthworms monitored and compared air and soil temperatures, assessed leaves' shapes and thicknesses, and then responded appropriately by, when desirable, pulling suitable leaves by their narrowest part, whether that was the tip or base. Of course, the advantages of having a warm burrow were accompanied by the danger of being caught by a bird while pulling in the leaves, so

Darwin's work suggested that even a blind and deaf earthworm was capable of informed risk–benefit analysis.[6]

IF MODERN SCIENCE'S analysis of nature is mainly detached, it is also sporadic. (Today, most ecological studies are only funded for between three and five years, which makes accurately tracking long-term relationships difficult.) On the other hand, nature's analysis of itself is engaged and continuous. For example, earthworms are herm-aphrodite – appropriately Mercurial – and, mid coitus, they can assess and adapt to each other's sexual history. The traditional sciences also studied nature in an engaged and continuous fashion. One of its grand narratives is the zodiac and – like Darwin's theory of evolution – it also grew out of apparently disconnected details. But, critically, emotional connections between the observer and the observed were not severed when bringing together its many details.

The traditional sciences assume that all parts of nature are con-nected, and they embrace connections with human nature in all its richness, unconstrained by institutional conventions or protocols. The traditional sciences also see all nature as purposeful, and the purpose of natural analysis – whether by sleeping seeds or copulating worms – is to be of some service to the wider world. In such a teleo-logical universe, the service offered by each (seemingly) separate part of nature is to sustain all life across all nature. Earthworms could be seen as engaged in a continual soil service, just as we care for our cars with periodic garage services and may even attend to our souls with occasional religious services.

This month's zodiac sign is not an animal but a woman. She is either Persephone or Demeter, Persephone's mother, and she holds the earth's produce in her hand. In Latin, Demeter's name is Ceres, the origin of our word 'cereal', while the name of the constellation's brightest star, Spica, means 'ear of wheat'. Virgo marks the end of a half-year of expansion, material growth and reproduction. Her seeds feed us through the year's second half – Libra to Pisces – a period of contraction that acknowledges the place of death in life. But when life-forms fall, either in death or in sleep, helped by the humble worm, the earth comes up to greet them, promising rebirth.

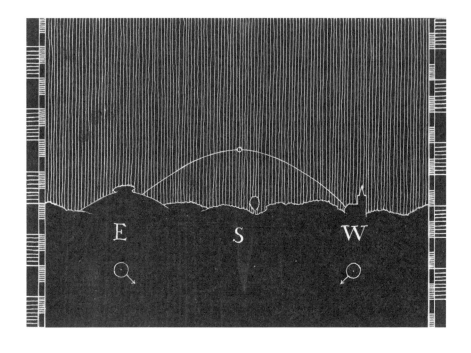

The Sun's path around the autumn equinox at a latitude of 52 degrees north.

Autumn Equinox

The word 'equinox' means 'equal night'. The equinox is that special time when the day and night are equally long, twelve hours each. The Autumn equinox occurs around 21 September, in the middle of the year's darkening half, when days are shortening and the length of night-time is increasing.

Unlike the solstices – which are easy to see from how the rising and setting Sun changes its position along the horizons – equinoxes are elusive. Their exact dates are difficult to determine because the length of day (and, of course, also night) changes fastest around the equinoxes. And, closer to the North or South Pole, gauging the lengths of days or nights becomes even more difficult. This is because, at the equator, the Sun comes straight up from the Earth and goes straight back down again, so night falls quickly. But, further from the equator, the rising Sun and the setting Sun appear and disappear gradually, increasingly skimming along the horizon. So, as we move through temperate zones towards poles, the twilight – the mysterious gloaming of dawn and dusk – grows and blurs the boundaries between day and night, known and unknown, times of the dog and the wolf.

Historically, many cultures just assumed the equinoxes were midway between solstices, as, in fact, within a few days, they are.[1]

Libra, based on star chart in Andreas Cellarius' *Harmonia Macrocosmica* (1661).

SEVEN

September–October
Cardinal Air, 'Journey to the Other'

This month sees the start of a new season, and each season is introduced by a different element. After fire (spring) and water (summer), air now introduces autumn when, according to John Clare, 'liquid gold is the air/ Whoever looks round sees eternity there' (*Autumn*). This is the time of year when we start becoming more aware of air, the vast theatre in which nature performs, the medium that envelops us, connecting yet also separating all of us. Now is when we can start to see our breath. And, since the Sun no longer ventures so high, its long shafts skim past shadows and pierce early-morning mists, sculpting the usually featureless space between us. We met air before in Gemini – in its mutable guise, disseminating information at the end of spring – but this is transformative cardinal air, the wind that blows away the summer to usher in the autumn.

Modern science says that winds happen because the Sun warms the Earth unevenly. On the other hand, Aristotle said that when the Sun warmed the Earth, it generated mixtures of wet and dry exhalations. Aristotle's elemental picture recalls the older, mythological image of Aeolus, who lived in a cave and kept his tightly bound bags of wind locked safely underground behind storm-proof doors, to be released only at the gods' bidding. So, in the zodiac, it is as if the last moments of the Sun's six-month dominance in earthy Virgo – immediately before the autumnal equinox – prompt the Earth to exhale in Libra. It's almost as if nature sighs at the end of a busy day's work, looking forward to a restful evening.

As a cardinal sign, Libra marks the start of a new relationship between the light and dark. The days continue to draw in and nights continue to grow, but now, having just passed the equinox – indiscernibly at first, then inexorably – darkness dominates. Libra's position in the zodiac is directly opposite Aries, which assertively announced the light half of the year, and Libra now introduces the dark half. The zodiac associates those born under this sign with the phrase 'I balance'. The other zodiac signs are all life-forms: animals, humans or hybrids, in keeping with the zodiac's etymological root, *zoe*, meaning life. But alone among constellations, Libra is represented by an artefact, a balance or set of scales. (In the ancient Greek zodiac, Libra's scales were still part of an animal – the twin pincers of next month's sign, Scorpio.)

A pair of scales immediately conjures the idea of relationships between different things on either side of the balance. Whether a market trader uses scales to weigh a bag of apples against a kilo, or Anubis weighs the heart of a deceased ancient Egyptian against Maat, the Feather of Truth, their intentions are the same. Scales or balances use the freedom permitted by movement within subtle, fluid air to determine a relationship between a known and an unknown. So, Libra's symbol could suggest that this is when we become more aware of nature's relationship with the unknown Other.

WHILE THE SLOWLY creeping cold helps make air seem more visible, now is also the time when nature's activities move off-stage and become less visible. The previous six months saw obvious material developments and, in Libra, the balance tips towards hidden spiritual developments. Heraclitus said that 'Nature loves to hide', and this month nature starts hiding herself under a cloak of darkness (*Fragment* B123). The next six months encourage us to acknowledge that nature in the Realm of Becoming is literally bewildering, reflecting a greater

Reality, beyond the Realm of Being, that can only be embraced through unknowing (*The Cloud of Unknowing*). Tracking nature through the dark half requires a willingness to meet the Other. Such encounters are the stuff of legend and one of them took place in a village about an hour from the table where I now sit and write.

AROUND THE YEAR 1200, an Augustinian canon and a Cistercian abbot both recorded eyewitness accounts of an incident at Woolpit, Suffolk.[1] After harvest time two small and bewildered children apparently emerged from an underground passage. They wore strange clothes, spoke an unknown language and had green skin. According to those accounts they gradually lost their colour upon, reluctantly, eating the food that villagers gave them. Some thought they were from the Land of Faerie, which was typically believed to be located beneath our world and to enjoy a different relationship with time, with decades that passed in seconds or with transposed – antipodean – seasons. Such encounters were once not uncommon and the Christian tradition accommodated fairies by seeing them as among those 'other sheep I have, which are not of this fold' (John 10:16). However, according to John Aubrey, fairies started to disappear from England in the seventeenth century (*Brief Lives*, II). Seventeenth-century speculations about Woolpit's green children – including those of a bishop – suggested that they may have fallen from the heavens and their skin changed colour after exposure to our air. (This suggests a connection with Libra's ruling planet, Venus, which is associated with copper, a metal that turns green in the air.[2]) So, the Otherworld's location can vary – either above us or below us – and it matters little whether we think of Otherworld stories as garbled facts, fairy tales or science fiction, since whatever position we take, there is always another position.

But how to get to the notoriously elusive Otherworld? Many journeys start with a wind, symbol of the moving spirit. For example, after ten years of war and nine days and nights of sailing, Odysseus was within sight of home when, greatly relieved, he fell asleep. An insubordinate crew took advantage of his slumbers and, in search of gold, opened a bag that had been a gift from Aeolus. Unfortunately, that bag contained a wind that blew them out to sea and started their epic wanderings (*Odyssey*, x). More recently, Dorothy – whose surname was Gale – was taken to the Land of Oz by a tornado. Her mode of transport followed a long tradition since, in the second century, Lucian of Samosata wrote about a Greek ship that sailed beyond the Pillars of Hercules – out of the Mediterranean and into the Atlantic – where it was caught in a whirlwind and ended up on the Moon (*A True Story*).

A spiralling wind is an apt symbol for the journey to the elusive Otherworld because it is disorienting and, to paraphrase that master of the winds, Cap'n Barbossa, you have to be lost to get to a place that can't be found (*Pirates of the Caribbean: At World's End*). And upon arrival, of course, you *are* lost – in wonder. Disorientation precedes reorientation, which is vital because change is inevitable. After all, even ants have to grapple with uncertainty, weighing up personal experience and social guidance when, for example, the location of food changes. Following stories of journeys to Otherworlds, we might imagine spiralling wind as the engine that turns the season, taking us from the year's light half to its dark half.

The North Atlantic hurricane season peaks around September and the – now-named, or re-personified – storms in which hurricanes grow are generally born in the East and return to the East to die. So, the part of the globe that created the zodiac rarely sees Kansas-style twisters. Europe's most common spirals of wind are hundreds of miles across and, while easy to see as cloud patterns in satellite images, they are invisible from ground level. Nonetheless, the way the winds turn has always provided important hints about what kind of weather the next days or weeks might bring. Because, just as the arms of a balance can twist clockwise or anticlockwise in the air, so too can the air itself turn both ways. Many whose lives and livelihoods depended on the weather – including John Claridge, the seventeenth-century Shepherd of Banbury – noted veering (clockwise) and backing (anticlockwise) winds that offered clues about what might lie unseen, over the horizon, days or weeks away. Yet while the air's own spirals are usually invisible, the air now houses other spirals that are visible.

SUDDENLY, SPIDERS' WEBS are everywhere. They come in all shapes and if we poke around we can find tangle, funnel, tube and sheet webs. But the ones that seem to actively present themselves to us – and therefore act as natural symbols – are orbs, or spirals. They are orderly, fit-for-purpose and have unity or identity, so are, in traditional terms, beautiful, especially when bedecked with dew. Spiders' obvious skills as structural engineers are complemented by their hidden skills as molecular engineers because spiders weave their webs from their own matter, consuming yesterday's web to make today's. They can produce seven or eight types of thread, each serving a different purpose. Some of the threads are stronger than steel and their properties depend on different molecular compositions – including combinations of protein nano-crystals and nano-springs – and different ways of spinning. Baby spiders, or spiderlings, make a single filament of silk that is drawn out of them by a gentle breeze. Held up by that thread, they are carried through the air by the wind – like Dorothy – and they start a new life wherever the thread gets caught, wherever the fates decree. Adult spiders spin lifelines and bridge-lines as well as the orb's rays, which are dry, and its spiral, which is sticky. The sticky threads trap the spider's prey while the dry threads allow her free movement and extend her senses, transmitting vibrations that help her identify what has been caught and where it is ensnared.[3]

Appropriately for creatures that seem to proliferate at the start of the year's dark half, spiders are associated with death and are attributes of Persephone, who disappeared into the Underworld in the autumn, like the seeds glorified in the constellation of Virgo. The ingenious spider also became the stuff of legend in her own right. For example, Ovid told of a human weaver, Arachne, who was so proud of her skills that she challenged the gods and, for her audacity, was turned into the world's very first spider (*Metamorphoses*, VI). Weaving symbolizes the world in a way that reinforces Libra's qualities since it involves the harmonious partnership of (at least) two different types of thread. The spider's sticky spiral is one long weft (or woof) thread, while the Other, dry rays, are many warp threads. Of course, the finished web is a single structure made of numerous joined threads, so it's an example of making one from many, which is of course a traditional definition of love, an attribute associated with Libra's ruler, Venus.

ALONG WITH SPIDERS, mushrooms also appear this month, suddenly, often seeming to pop up overnight. They are the only visible part of a life-form to which we will return in a couple of months, and they show themselves in our world now so that their spore can be carried by the wind, like ballooning spiderlings or pollen. (Fungal spores travel now, rather than when pollen travels, because, coming from the Otherworld, they like the damp and the dark so spring and summer's heat and light do not suit them.) Wild mushrooms and toadstools are highly sought after by those who know what they are looking for but, like spiders, they can have a bad reputation. In part, this is because some of them are edible, others are poisonous, and mistakes can prove fatal. However, in nature, things are rarely if ever black and white, and eating mushrooms can have a whole spectrum of possible consequences. Many of them, for example, have psychoactive qualities and ingesting them is another time-honoured way of accessing Otherworlds.

Mushrooms' overnight appearance can also take us back to one particular Otherworld, the Land of Faerie. On pastures, mushrooms sprout up in September and October, growing in rings which can expand over the years to reach tens of metres in diameter. Traces of these fairy circles or fairy rings endure long after the mushrooms have disappeared, and are sought after by grazing animals for their luxuriant grasses. Along with other natural markers, these circles of rich grass – with or without the mushrooms that helped create them – traditionally identify entrances to the Otherworld. They are protected in many cultures for fear of reprisal from disgruntled fairies, trolls or Otherfolk.[4]

The visible mushroom is an ephemeral fruiting body and, like many plant pollens, its spores are usually invisible. Yet, unlike spores, many wind-blown seeds actually can be seen in the air at this time of year. Big, heavy sycamore seeds, for example, have large wings that help them travel further from the mother tree, spiralling down and catching the wind, floating like helicopters. Whether spiderling, spore or seed, being blown by the wind is like being transported by the spirit to new life. As the Bible says, 'The wind blows where it wishes, and you hear the sound of it, but cannot tell where it comes from and where it goes' (John 3:7–8).

ACTUALLY, ARISTOTLE THOUGHT he could tell where the wind came from. He said it came from the earth, like Aeolus' winds. And, since trees also come from the earth, when the wind takes a seed from a tree and carries it to earth, it is part of a circular journey. Both the seed and the wind are returning to where they came from. This circularity, joining beginning and end, is one – possibly disorienting – manifestation of the mystical conjunction of opposites. Just as the opposite elements, earth and air, just met over the autumn equinox, so opposite elements, water and fire, will meet over the spring equinox. The marriage of (hot and dry) fire and (cold and wet) water had visible expression through the spring and summer, the seasons dominated by light. Now, the marriage of (cold and dry) earth and (hot and wet) air will have invisible consequences through the autumn and winter, the seasons dominated by darkness.

So, circling – or, acknowledging the flow of time, spiralling – from earth to air and back again encourages us to reorient and respond to expectations that can be turned upside down upon entering the dark half of the year. For example, last month apples fell, and there is a saying that 'an apple never falls far from the tree,' implying that children are like their parents. But sycamore seeds are good counterexamples because, thanks to their wings, they can indeed 'fall far from the tree', yet they are no less like their parents. In other words, the example of sycamore seeds balances the proverbial example of apples to show – in typically Libran fashion – that there are always two sides to any story. And, even if a plant seed is eaten by a bird, there might still be two sides to the story of its ongoing journey through the world.

Obviously, one possible fate for the seed is that it is thoroughly digested and thereby sacrifices its own potential for life in order to sustain the life of another. In the autumn of a 'mast' year, when oaks are especially fruitful, a single blue jay can collect and bury thousands of acorns as its winter food-store. Jays are very selective about where they plant their acorns and remember their locations well but, if a bird dies over the harsh winter, the acorns it buried may grow, sometimes a kilometre (⅔ mi.) or so from the mother tree.[5] Of course, if the acorn escaped being eaten by the jay, then there are still two sides to its ongoing journey because, rather than growing, it could rot. And even if a seed is eaten, that need not be the end of its story, either. For example, the mistletoe – which, as the 'golden bough', was said to have helped Aeneas gain access to the Underworld (*Aeneid*, VI) – produces seeds that can germinate after passing through the gut of a bird like the mistle thrush. The mistletoe was sacred to Druids because it was evergreen (so apparently undying), grew into a sphere (which is the perfect shape) and lived in oaks (which are the king of trees, although it must be said that mistletoe seem less picky about their hosts today). Sticky mistletoe seeds also got stuck to or eaten by birds, then brushed off their beaks, or excreted, on to tree boughs. This enabled the undying and perfectly shaped mistletoe to complete its life cycle without ever touching the ground, making it a truly aerial, or heavenly, plant. This month mistletoe starts making its presence felt, appearing after the wind has blown away the host's veil of leaves.

THE FACT THAT THE MISTLETOE WAS ON THE TREE all year long but is only revealed by leaf fall mirrors the fact that stars are in the sky all day long but are hidden by sunlight and only revealed by nightfall. Both the hidden mistletoe and the hidden stars suggest that the Otherworld is always present, even though we may often be unable to see it. Present but unperceived phenomena suggest that if we let our perception adjust, the dark half of the year might show us things that we miss through the light half of the year. Mistletoe may become visible in the autumn, as stars become visible in the dark, but – more in keeping with everyday expectations – the acorns buried by a jay all become invisible by moving from our world of light to a world of darkness. Out of sight, they continue through time, possibly being dug up and eaten by the jay, or maybe being left to take root or rot. One way or another, they ride or drive the cycle of life.

In the parable of the sower it was said that some seeds fall on 'good ground' and prosper while others do not (Matthew 13:18–23). This stark binary might seem reinforced by Libra's sign – which can evoke either innocence or guilt – but there are, in fact, many ways of balancing the scales. What is 'good' for one seed may not be good for another and – as jay-friendly acorns, mistletoe and sycamore show – there are many ways of finding good ground. If winged seeds like sycamore fall on 'good' ground, then their aerial journey ends there because further progress is stopped by getting caught up in the existing covering of plants. So, they take root where they find themselves. However, if they land on stony ground, there is nothing to stop them continuing their wind-blown journey and, the more barren the terrain, the further they go. This is how trees regenerate the scarred land left by retreating glaciers, for example, windsurfing many miles of bare rock until they find a detritus-filled corner in which to put down roots. This is difficult for most of us to see in the wild, because most winged seeds will have been blown off the smooth stone to lie hidden among the plants of more receptive, or 'good', terrain. But windsurfing seeds are easy to see in cities where, for an autumnal week or so, sycamore seeds skate down streets and pavements to gather in gutters or corners. This is why, in conker season, children can also find and play with nature's helicopters. However, it is unlikely that an urban child's natural helicopter will grow into a sycamore tree. For seeds of all types, life is in the balance.

It follows that encounters with the Other can seem hostile, and nature's approach to the apparently hostile Other is, in biblical terms, to turn the other cheek (Luke 6:29). The zodiac recognizes that life's continuity does not hang on the fate of any individual but on the selfless fulfilment of diverse – and potentially fatal – roles within multispecies communities. In the feminine sign, Taurus, Venus showed her love, harmony and beauty. Here, in a masculine sign, her power and mystery have different qualities. There is still love, but it might seem tough love. There is still harmony, but it might come at a cost. And there is still beauty, but it might take time or distance to show itself. The two pans in Libra's scales are reminders that following the cycle of life can require us to change our focus.

Scorpio, based on star chart in Andreas Cellarius' *Harmonia Macrocosmica* (1661).

EIGHT

October–November
Fixed Water, 'Dwelling in Darkness'

Scorpio is the fixed sign at the centre of autumn, when the descent into darkness feels at its most intense. Scorpio is another water sign and the idea of combining 'fixed' and 'water' might seem to suggest stagnation, but everything is connected through the year, so, although still, Scorpio's fixed water is still flowing. This month is like an enormous lake of unfathomable depth, at the bottom of which matter putrefies and decomposes, lying in such darkness that none can tell where anything begins or ends. Still water's power lies in its irresistible ability to dissolve all boundaries and oppositions.

The mirror-like surface of still water faithfully reflects the heavens, but if we venture through that looking-glass we can drown. Water is the stuff of life, but it's also the realm of the dead. Last month, life started moving through the air towards the Other and, in this watery sign, we arrive at our destination. After all, Odysseus was tested by both wind and water, and crossing water can symbolize accessing the Other since the souls of the dead are ferried across the River Styx. In fact, many historic accounts of personal journeys to the Otherworld have much in common with modern accounts of near-death experiences.[1] The year's focus has now changed. This sign focuses on death and loss of identity, and – because Scorpio is fixed – its focus is unwavering.

On the other hand, the unwavering focus of modern science has not yet securely settled on death. Of course, modern science continues the ancient Martial tradition of developing technologies that deliver death. And, in the chemical warfare of modern food produc-tion, modern science has industrialized the delivery of death to those that – through no fault of their own – have been turned into weeds and pests by monocultures. Modern science also continues the ancient medical traditions associated with death's natural approach, the end of life, by developing new methods of palliative care. Yet death itself, and what happens after it, is still largely a closed book for modern science. Nonetheless, as far as bodies are concerned – following death through misadventure or foul play – forensic science establishes iden-tities through traces of DNA. Forensic science also establishes times of death through the creatures that feast on corpses, since distinct sequences of organisms are involved in decomposition. We might therefore expect ecologists to have some interest in life after death, and they do, at least, know where it happens.

Central to the ecological worldview is a food web that consists of two equally important interwoven pathways. These are the 'grazing', green-world or above-ground food chain (building up from the living) and the 'detrital', brown-world or below-ground food chain (breaking down of the dead).[2] For aeons, these two pathways have been perfectly synchronized by ever-changing successions of diverse communities – composed of insects, fungi, microbes and so on – that recycle dead plants and animals with extraordinary efficiency.

The sea urchin's roles in kelp forests hint at the complexity of interactions between the grazing and detrital pathways. If urchins' populations are not checked by otters, their grazing is catastrophic for kelp forests and the micro-organisms that live there. But, in healthy forests, urchins can be beneficial since they eat detached pieces of kelp that would otherwise drift out of the forest. In the presence of urchins, these pieces are shredded so that nutritious detritus – urchin faeces and tiny fragments of dead kelp – locally feeds more micro-organisms.[3] In turn, those creatures become the basis of other grazing food chains. So, sea urchins can play ecologically constructive as well as destructive roles. The dynamics and mechanisms that govern interactions between the detrital and grazing chains – the necrobiome – are subtle and complex and, to date, they have received relatively little joined-up attention from ecologists.[4]

That neglect may not be too surprising since people may, understandably, not want to devote their working lives to studying what most of us find repulsive, like the continued activities of gut bacteria that bloat roadkill on the motorway hard shoulder. More fundamentally, many still labour under the shadow of twentieth-century taboos about death. The detrital pathway is, after all, a great leveller. A human corpse is food, just like any other corpse.

On the other hand, over the last fifty years, social scientists have noted a significant shift in Western attitudes towards death. Death continues to mark the end of the body but, as far as the mind is concerned, it is now increasingly seen as a gateway to other realities.[5] Of course, the mysterious alchemy of life after death has always had a healthy place in religion and mythology. In the premodern world, the mind and body – or, more accurately, body and soul – were seen as intimately entwined in a reality made jointly of spirit and matter. Some modern scientists may still believe in the soul personally, but their beliefs have no place in the laboratory, so they follow Darwin in leading split lives.

A TIME WILL come to dwell upon the soul. But for now we can just acknowledge the zodiac as being constructed from cosmic and mythic relationships that parallel nature's interwoven grazing and detrital pathways. Life and death ceaselessly interact with each other in the extraordinarily thin margin between the heavens and the Underworld, and the liminal biosphere's exchanges are driven alternately from above, visibly, and below, obscurely. Taking turns from one month to the next, the drivers from above are traditionally masculine or active, either fire or air, while those from below are feminine or receptive, either water or earth. As fixed water, Scorpio is feminine and it lies directly opposite the zodiac's other fixed feminine sign, Taurus, or fixed earth.[6] Spring's Taurus was a time of having, while autumn's Scorpio is a time of loss, or not having. So, as the reflection of Taurus, the zodiac associates those born under this sign with the phrase 'I desire'. Appropriately in the context of the zodiac, the word 'desire' comes from the Latin *desiderare*, which probably means 'awaiting what the stars will bring', from *de sidere*, or 'of the stars'. Above all, at the slowly cooling heart of autumn, we desire life, and the desire to maintain life in the face of death is one of nature's most powerful forces.

The year's descent into darkness is essential before any upward return to the light is possible. After all, death to the world precedes birth to the spirit. As the Bible put it, 'If it die, it bringeth forth much fruit' (John 12:24). Death is the destruction of the old order and is a necessary step towards creating a new order. In the zodiac, that sacrifice is assisted by Scorpio's ruling planet, Mars, which works inwardly – making many from one – indiscriminately dismembering all identifiable life-forms and generating a rich anonymous humus. The passage from Taurus to Scorpio could be summed up by the Bible's 'He cometh forth like a flower and is cut down' (Job 14:2).

The coming months that will eventually lead back to flowers' re-appearance as emerging shoots all involve obscure, hidden activities. This is when trees' sap seems to slip effortlessly underground, descending into the lower realms for the dark half of the year, before being drawn back up by the Sun next spring. Over the next few months, the Underworld will enrich that sap, preparing it for its life-giving role when it returns to our world. And, given that sap is plants' life-blood, the annual cycle of life could be compared with the flow of our own blood. Autumn could then be seen to represent the start of the heart's diastole phase, when the heart relaxes and fills with blood, after the active pumping contraction of the systole phase. The last six months were dominated by heavenly light that offered us mind-like clarity about life. But now, through the six months dominated by Otherworldly darkness, life is channelled – like diastolic blood – through the dark, hidden chambers of the heart and its dream-like mysteries.

Traditionally, blood also featured in agriculture this month because, although Scorpio's labours of the month included sowing seeds, it was also when farmers brought their herds down from the pastures and slaughtered surplus stock. The Christian tradition marked this time with the Dance Macabre and Dance of the Dead. While those customs probably became more popular in response to the great plague, the Black Death, their place in the calendar faithfully reflects life's apparent retreat through October and November. A pale shadow of those full-blooded celebrations limps on in today's Halloween.

In nature, some trees signal this period of blood-letting by themselves turning the colour of blood. Modern science explains the change from green to red leaves in terms of the degradation of chlorophyll, which is no longer needed for photosynthesis, and the production of anthocyanins, which slow the rate of cell death in leaves. According to some scientists, it is a sign that trees are recycling nutrients as they shut down for the winter.

Traditional sciences also explain those changes but do not 'explain them away'. Instead, out of respect for nature, they preserve and enhance its mystery, providing the order we crave, but not at nature's expense. So, the redness of autumnal leaves – and berries – could traditionally be seen as the sign of the accumulation of the Sun's fire over the summer, like the final expression of the process that started with Leo's ripening apples. Of course, red is also part of spring's palette, but springtime and autumnal reds differ, just as the red skies of dawn and dusk differ. Springtime and morning reds seem fresh and alert, announcing the coming year or day. On the other hand, autumnal and evening reds seem more relaxed, basking in the satisfaction of a year, or day, well spent. In keeping with Scorpio's blood-letting, autumn's weathered red is more like the dull, stale blood that can flow from broken veins, while spring's renewed red is like the bright, enriched blood that flows from ruptured arteries.

♏

MYTHOLOGICALLY, THESE SYNCHRONIZED alternating rhythms – like the grazing and detrital pathways, or active systole and relaxed diastole – were reflected through the course of the whole year by the fate of Virgo's Persephone. She was abducted and taken into the Underworld in the autumn, made Queen, wedded to Hades, and returned to her family above ground in the spring, spending – according to Ovid – half a year in each realm (*Metamorphoses*, v). Travelling from the light of our world and needing to navigate the Underworld's darkness, Persephone must have paused to let her eyes adjust.

Scorpio's still waters, whose surface reflects whatever is above, offer another opportunity to pause and adjust our eyes. According to Ovid, it was the watery vision from above that appealed to Narcissus. The beautiful but proud son of a 'dark river nymph' cruelly rebuffed countless admirers until he glimpsed his own reflection in a tranquil pool. Transfixed, he fell in love with his borrowed likeness, which seemed to reciprocate his every move and mood. Reaping what he had sown, he was, of course, cruelly rebuffed by the ungraspable object of his affections. Nonetheless, he stayed rooted to the spot and eventually faded away, his only remaining trace being the flower that bears his name (*Metamorphoses*, III). However, completely overlooked by Narcissus, still waters also offer glimpses of what lies below. Still water's surface is obviously not disturbed by waves to break up the image from above but, maybe less obviously, neither is its body stirred up with sediment to cloud the image from below. The deeper the water, the darker the image and, as the Bible says, 'He discovereth deep things out of darkness' (Job 12:22).

Scorpio is a time of losing identities and the story of Narcissus hints at the dangers of clinging to individual identities that are, inevitably, limited. At least occasionally, most of us manage to recognize that life is fleeting and that we need to break away from self-absorption, turning our attention to others. The poet John Keats, for example, loved Fanny Brawne very deeply, but he also knew that their connection – dependent on ephemeral identities – was an inevitably brief and passing affair. The epitaph on his grave reads, 'Here lies one whose name was writ in water.' Looking beyond the surface illusions of individual identities opens up the possibility of discovering 'deep things out of darkness' in the mysteries of this half of the year. Having turned the corner towards darkness last month, separate identities are now slipping away, like scattered leaves or buried acorns, and one way to understand nature's continued activity is to recognize, and avoid, Narcissus' fixation on surface appearances.

In the Christian tradition, Adam and Eve's limited understanding of identity and their self-centred behaviour caused the earth's taste for blood, as well as the sweat now needed to access her riches (Genesis 4:10–11 and 3:17–19). Being able to see beyond one's own self requires a transformation of our everyday approach to life and such tearing away from self-interest and surface appearances was evidently beyond the capabilities of Narcissus. In fact, it is so radical that the possibility is sometimes not even recognized. And, appropriately in the context of the year's descent into the Underworld, the word 'radical' means 'of the roots'. The truly radical is therefore only noticed after it has managed to create growth above ground, and most who claim to be radical are merely tinkering with what has already emerged. On the other hand, the dark half of the year is truly – and routinely – radical since, in the zodiac, it represents the unnoticed ways in which life overcomes death.

Unrecognized radical behaviour also occurred in the story of two sisters who offered Jesus hospitality. One sister busied herself with preparing and serving food while the other just sat, watched and listened. When the busy sister asked Jesus to rebuke her seemingly lazy sister, he replied, 'thou art careful and troubled about many things, but one thing is needful' (Luke 10:41–2). That 'one thing needful' is exactly what nature encourages of us through the dark half of the year, when the reaping is over, the sowing is done and there is little to do but sit, watch, listen and wait.

WAITING IN SCORPIO's still water encourages the contemplation of big questions such as: who are we and what happens to us after death?

In the premodern world, such questions inspired many great works of literature. For example, in his *Divine Comedy*, Dante journeyed through the nine circles of Hell before scaling Mount Purgatory and arriving in Paradise. The poet's trajectory – descent into darkness, followed by ascent into the light – has obvious parallels with the trajectory of seeds, whether sown by farmers or scattered by winds. Yet, unlike agriculture or nature – where seed follows seed, year after year – Dante's journey was a one-off affair, in keeping with the Christian tradition's conception of a time that runs in a straight line from the Creation to the Day of Judgement. However, ideas about our posthumous fate that have a more cyclical character, and are therefore more like nature, also once circulated across Europe.

For example, in his comments on the ancient Druids' beliefs, the Roman poet Lucan said, 'If their tale be true, death is but a point in the midst of continuous life' (*Pharsalia*, 1, 458). Lucan's 'continuous life' was the string of repeated lives enjoyed by one soul incarnating again and again through many bodies, each death simply being when the soul travelled from one bodily vehicle to another. Fragments of the Druids' oral doctrine of soul-transfer, or metempsychosis, are alluded to in the fourteenth-century Irish *Yellow Book of Lecan*. In a seventeenth-century history of Britain, the English poet Michael Drayton hoped that the Druids' doctrine was true so that he might harbour the soul of an ancient bard in his breast (*Poly Olbion*, 1, i). And for another seventeenth-century English poet, John Donne, the soul's circuitous progress was still eventually heaven-bound – and driven by wind on water – since, 'though through many straits and lands I roam/ I launch at Paradise and sail toward home' (*Metempsychosis*, 56–7).

Metempsychosis, the European version of reincarnation, certainly pre-dates Pythagoras, but it became widely associated with him through Ovid's summary of his teachings. For Pythagoras, souls were immortal and, upon death, were 'received into new homes', sometimes human and sometimes other-than-human. For that reason, he promoted a vegetarian diet, reminding his listeners that the people of the Golden Age did not 'defile their lips with blood'.[7] Again, according to Ovid, Pythagoras suggested that, accompanying the transmigration of souls – which were 'as pliable as wax' – there was also a transmigration of bodies. He said that bees sprang from the corpses of oxen, and bees made 'thyme-scented honey' because they inherited their 'devotion to toil' from the ox. Hornets, however, got their aggression from the dead war-horses in which they were born (*Metamorphoses*, xv).[8] The ox that pulled the plough was a nursery-in-waiting for bees, so animals were somehow hosts to other animals. But not all animals are visible.

♏︎

MODERN SCIENCE MAY be largely silent about life after death, but it has much to say about who we are in life. In 1676, using his innovative home-made microscope, Antoni van Leeuwenhoek saw swarms of tiny animals – each a hundred times smaller than a grain of sand – in a single drop of rainwater. His report to the Royal Society of London caused 'considerable merriment' and 'giggling', and was rejected. It took science over three hundred years to recognize that those microbes are an integral part of who we think we are.

In the last two decades, other technological advances have enabled the rapid identification of such microbes in complex communities, or microbiomes, in every conceivable environment.[9] And, as far as microbes are concerned, we offer conceivable, habitable environments.

Each human hosts some 100 trillion bacteria, with our lower gut alone containing about 30,000 different species, twice as many as there are in an acre of undisturbed tropical rainforest. In fact, our bodies offer environments as diverse as savannah, swamp, sea and sky, and the populations of microbes on the skin, for example, are different on and inside the elbow, between the eyebrows, behind the ears and under the armpit. But, unlike populations within global ecosystems, which change with the seasons and over the years, microbiome populations can change over minutes and hours. Distinct mixes of microbes also live in the mouth, throat, nose, hair, stomach and vagina. They are an inseparable part of us. The number of genes in human DNA – 20,000 – is dwarfed by our microbiome's 5 to 8 million genes. These microbial communities are essential for our health; they are influenced by our states of mind and, in turn, they influence our minds.[10]

These invisible creatures live with us, on us and in us. Of course, some of them can cause diseases to which we may or may not be immune. Yet it seems that immune systems do not protect an individual from attack. Rather, immunity is now becoming seen as an expression of the balance between the self, a human, and the non-self, a microbe. (Likewise, in agriculture, pests and weeds are not inherently harmful but are made so by the imbalance of monocultures.) It follows that the self is not fixed and different from the Other, but is in flux, constantly redefining itself in its dialogue with the Other.

Those who planted the seeds of modern science – including van Leeuwenhoek – saw themselves as autonomous, independent individuals. And modern science began to see the things it studied – including, eventually, van Leeuwenhoek's tiny animals – as also being autonomous, independent individuals. But today, just as social scientists report a change in attitudes over the last fifty years about what happens to us after death, so those working in the biological sciences report a change in attitudes about what we are in life. It turns out we have never been individuals.[11]

All things have their seasons and the modern biological and environmental sciences seem engaged in an autumnal transformation. It is as if Scorpio's still waters are helping dissolve nineteenth- and twentieth-century science's boundaries and oppositions between the self and non-self, the human and other-than-human.

Sagittarius, based on star chart in Andreas Cellarius' *Harmonia Macrocosmica* (1661).

NINE

November–December
Mutable Fire, 'Sharing Wealth'

The previous month focused on loss of identity and death, so this sign should focus on what follows death, although of course, the 'Spoiler of worldly mansions' stalks the globe all year round (*Tales from the Thousand and One Nights*). However, there are rhythms within rhythms and the zodiac represents logical as well as temporal relationships. So, it makes perfect sense for the zodiac to acknowledge death's role in the cycle of life at a time when darkness descends, when leaves fall and when some birds – which generally represent the soul – have flown. Swallows, for instance, will probably have started their journey to other lands – in their case, South Africa – early in the sign of cardinal air.

Setting aside concerns about the soul for now, how does life continue after death? For those who are left behind, life continues around a gap that may be difficult or impossible to fill. But the deceased themselves actually fill gaps in the lives of others. If buried, their bodies become food for the worms. If cremated, their flesh mainly becomes water and carbon dioxide that might be breathed in by a growing tree, while about half of the remaining 2 or 3 kilograms (4½–6½ lbs) of ash are phosphorus, which is a mineral that is essential for plant growth.

One way or another, life thrives on consuming the dead. But it can be a slow process, and this is reflected in the zodiac's ruling planet. Last month was ruled by Mars, whose orbit was less than two Earth years, while this month is ruled by Jupiter, whose orbit is about twelve Earth years. (The orbit of next month's ruler, Saturn, will be nearly thirty Earth years.) All nature's processes through late autumn and the winter months are slow – even those associated with new life – and they are usually hidden, like the changes that are taking place in pregnant ewes, between conceiving in Scorpio and giving birth in Aries.

As the father of the gods, Jupiter is traditionally characterized by expansive largesse, benevolence and exchange. Earlier in the year, two other months were also characterized by exchange, personified by Gemini's pollinators and Virgo's earthworms. Both those signs were also mutable – at the end of spring and summer, respectively – and they distributed riches ready for the next season. Both were also in the light half of the year and were ruled by fast-moving Mercury, associated with relatively rapid and local exchanges. In the dark half of the year, Jupiter's slow orbit is associated with steadier, long-term exchanges at the end of autumn.[1] And, appropriately, the unhurried exchanges that happen after death mainly take place in the Underworld's darkness. Although life in the Earth extends down to a depth of around 3 kilometres (2 mi.), we will stay in the shallows of subterranean life, around the same depth as the worms and the acorns buried by jays. This often-overlooked slice of the biosphere is where the grazing and detrital pathways usually meet. Last month's harvest festivals celebrated crops, which are the foundation of grazing pathways, but nature's Jovian benevolence also extends to the detrital pathway's less obvious bounty.

Mutable Sagittarius is a fire sign. This is fire's third and final appearance in the year. It opened spring, was at the heart of summer and now closes autumn. Fire has no place in the winter that is just around the corner, and its current role is to gently slow-cook food for next year. Of course, like death, that slow-cooking happens all year round, but it's easier to see right now, since the modest heat of decomposition is lost in the summer's radiant heat, just as ever-present starlight is lost in sunlight. Sagittarian decomposition raises trees as fermentation raises bread, and the heat of hidden decomposition causes steam to rise from the compost heaps of any well-managed late autumn allotment or garden.

WHEN SNAKE VENOM coursed through Cleopatra's veins and she felt herself rising up to the heavens, she triumphantly claimed, 'I am fire, and air; my other elements/ I give to baser life' (*Antony and Cleopatra*, v, ii). The 'baser life' that took Cleopatra's 'other elements' – her water and earth – includes the invisibly small creatures that make up soil's microbiome. After Mars' strife made many from one in watery Scorpio, the process of reduction continues at an even finer scale in fiery Sagittarius. Fire may seem to consume bodies but, in reality, it just penetrates and divides them, then redistributes the pieces, like the logs of wood on a hearth that become the smoke and soot that go up the chimney.

Upwardly mobile fire is the brightest, subtlest element and is usually associated with the heavens. However, there is also a long cosmological tradition of fire at the centre of the Earth. Subterranean fire lay behind the heat that miners encountered deep underground – it heated hot springs and, occasionally, it escaped in volcanos, homeward bound, the fiery equivalent of a particularly vigorous bubble of air in water. The presence of this real subterranean fire reinforced the idea of the mythical fires of hell.

The cold, damp soil of November and December may not seem an obvious hiding place for fire. After all, last month's waters helped grass to regain the emerald-green glitter it had lost through the Dog Days. But the cycle of life is full of mystery and appearances can be deceptive. For example, somewhere in the East, someone discovered that soil contained a dramatic hidden inner fire. At first it was only used in firecrackers to celebrate births, marriages and funerals – rituals to mark stages in the cycle of life – but by the eleventh century it was turned into an incendiary weapon. By the fourteenth century, knowledge of it spread to Europe, where, as saltpetre, it was turned into an explosive and became the hidden force inside cannons and guns. Saltpetre was combined with sulphur – also known as brimstone, thus associated with the mythical fires of hell – together with charcoal, to make gunpowder. This subterranean concoction usurped the yew tree's longbows to become the preferred way of delivering death from a distance. Seventeenth-century English alchemists had exotic names for this mysterious soil extract, including the 'spirit of the earth' and 'universal sperm', although Shakespeare thought that what had been 'torn from the bowels of the harmless earth' just deserved to be called 'villainous' (*1 Henry IV*, I, iii).

This fiery spirit of the earth – now called potassium nitrate – was extracted from earth that had been soiled by urine and dung. Ironically, given its military application, it was often associated with the droppings of doves and commonly sought from the earth around dovecotes. Traditional science understood saltpetre as the natural distillation of a residual life-force that was found in rotting excrement and dead bodies. And that understanding of saltpetre would have been reinforced by the fact that it can also form the pure white crystals that sometimes grow, like very fine hoar frost, low on the inside of church walls and across church floors. To members of the congregation, it would have seemed as if refined portions of their buried ancestors had quietly crept out of their graves and seeped through the earth, and then the walls and floors, to join their descendants in the nave.

Unseen by anyone, the spirit of the earth, universal sperm, saltpetre or potassium nitrate was helped on its way from grave to nave by the human microbiome, the necrobiome and a soil microbiome that contained nitrogen-fixing bacteria. But saltpetre is unusual. It is a mineral that is liberated by microbes and naturally makes its way to church unless diverted to feed armaments. The overwhelming majority of minerals that are liberated by microbes stay within the cycle of life. And what keeps them circulating there are some creatures that can be truly gigantic, even if they are very, very different from the giants of legend. Those creatures may be enormous, but they are also very well hidden and, like plankton-grazing great whales, their appetite is confined to extremely small things.

BY NOW, FALLEN leaves are rotting down and becoming one with the earth. Meanwhile, the trees have become completely skeletal and can look so arresting against the late autumn sky that their image has helped structure people's interpretations of the world. Some conceptual trees, like the mythical Norse world-tree Yggdrasil, include roots. However, most just focus on the visible branches. Modern versions include Darwinian 'evolutionary trees' and information technology's 'decision trees'. These graphic structures imply hierarchies – trunks come first, then limbs, branches and lastly twigs and leaves – and they encourage thinking about the world in terms of binaries, since each junction represents an either/or choice.

Through the 1970s and '80s, those hierarchies and binaries caused some philosophers to fall out with trees. Instead, they preferred to see the world with the help of a different metaphor – also drawn from the natural world – the tangled underground, interconnected, web-like networks called rhizomes. In fact, the mainly visible, vertical trees and the mainly hidden, horizontal rhizomes are both valid ways of thinking about relationships between things in the world. Moreover, in nature, trees and rhizome-like fungi are intimately connected, suggesting that our metaphors should not be 'either trees or rhizomes', but instead, 'both trees and rhizomes'. The connection between trees and rhizome-like structures – each facilitated by their microbiomes – shows how life overcomes death.

But, for over a century, our understanding of the natural world has been shaped by Darwin's assumption that life-forms were individuals that competed with each other, with only the fittest surviving. So, it's easy for us to see how soil fungi could infect and kill seeds and saplings and therefore regulate plant numbers, just like grazing by insects or animals. Yet now, by looking beyond the limited roles of individuals, ecologists see that – by killing some seeds – soil fungi make room for other plants to grow, thus promoting plant diversity. The death of one plant directly enables the life of another plant, one whose roots are less prone to attack by that particular fungus.

It might seem reasonable to expect that a tree's roots extend as far as its branches, enabling them to collect water from far and wide, just as leaves collect light from far and wide. But it is much easier to grow through the subtle air than it is to grow through the dense earth, and it would take lots of energy to extend roots as far as branches. Also, just because a tree can look as if it is alone above ground, we might assume that it is also alone below ground. In fact, it is not. What is visible is not always a straightforward guide to what is not visible.

TREE ROOTS ROUTINELY share the soil with all sorts of fungus. Some may kill seeds and saplings, but many are beneficial. Fungi are not plants or animals, and while they may look more like plants, they are actually more like animals. Relations between plants and fungi are sometimes parasitic, with one taking advantage of the other and offering nothing in exchange, but the overwhelming majority of plants – including most trees and grasses – engage in mutually beneficial relationships with fungi. Most of these beneficial mycorrhizal fungi actively penetrate plants' roots with microscopic structures to assist their exchanges. A few wrap themselves around plants' roots, and they include the types that produced the fairy rings that briefly raised their fruiting bodies in Libra. Both types of fungus grow extremely fine rhizome-like, branching hyphae that form complex networks, or mycelia, which vastly extend the plant's root system.

Microscopic fossil evidence suggests that the entangled relationships between plants and fungi go back 400 million years and their success rests upon cooperation and collaboration, not on competition. A tree would find it hard to grow its relatively thick roots through earth, but the much finer mycorrhizal networks spread much more easily, exploring more territory and accessing more nutrients. In fact, it has been said that mycorrhizas, not roots, are the way that most land plants get most of their nutrients. Fungi also benefit from trees because they cannot make carbohydrates, like sugar. In fact, up to a third of the sugar that trees create can go into feeding their fungal partners. In return, fungi digest the remains of the dead and rocks to provide the tree with essential minerals, including phosphorus from bone and nitrogen from salmon, while chlorophyll's magnesium comes from solid rock, like dolomite. Mycorrhizal relationships involve swapping plant-produced sugars and fungus-sourced minerals.[2] That mutually beneficial exchange of stuff from the heavens (sugars made from air and fiery sunlight) and stuff from the Underworld (earthy minerals dissolved in water) is completely consistent with the character of Sagittarius' ruling planet, Jupiter.

The extraordinary size and longevity of forest fungal networks are only now beginning to be uncovered. For example, in a Michigan forest, a single network more than 1,500 years old extends over the area of several football pitches and it has been estimated that – theoretically, since it would be impossible to disentangle it from its home – it would weigh around 100,000 kilograms (220,460 lbs), the equivalent of a blue whale. Yet that particular network is dwarfed by one in an Oregon forest which extends over 8 square kilometres (3 sq. mi.), interacting with thousands of trees and estimated to be between 2,000 and 9,000 years old. This stately yet unseen creature was probably alive when Aristotle was sauntering around Greece. It has survived thousands of years in terrains that have been naturally transformed by fires, by floods, by landslips and by the arrival of new species of animals, plants and microbes. It has successfully adapted to all those disturbances, many of which are now amplified by climate change. (Further underground, life is less influenced by change, so deep life is constant unless disrupted by intrusive human activities like fracking and ground-water extraction.)

With networks of such grand scale and age it is not surprising that the tree–fungus relationship is not exclusive or one-to-one. Although silent and slow-moving, the fungus has enormous freedom and explores its habitat to go wherever it sees fit. One fungus therefore has relationships with many trees and one tree can likewise have relationships with many fungi. The spreading network of trees and fungi weaves together and connects many creatures in a completely entangled and open-ended labyrinthine mosaic. Even without considering local microbiomes, interdependencies in these vast webs further blur the boundaries of what constitutes an individual.

YET THE COMPLEX half-hidden infrastructure that supports life – even through death – does much more than just swap sugars and salts. It is also a communications network that enables numerous different types of shorter-term exchange. Each 'individual' tree has its own communication network; for example, the plant hormones auxin and cytokinin coordinate the growth of shoots and roots, respectively, so that trees can balance their rates of harvesting sunlight from above with minerals from below. Yet communication also takes place between different trees, so that an insect attack on one tree prompts the release of pheromones that alert other trees to the threat. However, like an orchid's fragrance or moth's pheromone, tree's airborne messages are only carried downwind. A tree's other chemical messages can flow in every direction to other trees via the underground mycorrhizal networks. So, in less than a day, the neighbours of an attacked or infected plant can mount their defences thanks to stress signals delivered through these underground networks. The fungal networks therefore help the plants, but they can also recognize a hopeless case and transfer minerals away from a dying tree, for example, redirecting scarce resources to heathy neighbours. Trees coordinate their synchronized fruiting through these networks and those that discourage the growth of others also use them to extend their inhibiting influence.

Fungi feed orchids early in their lives and, when the orchids reach maturity, most of them return the favour to feed fungi. Plants defend their fungal networks from species that threaten them, and mature trees use them to give support to young saplings. Other fungi facilitate two-way traffic of food and drink between different plants in seasonal flows that are like vast invisible underground tides.

Following Darwin, most modern scientists have the reputation of trying not to think about the things they study in human terms, but mycorrhizal networks have encouraged some scientists to follow those philosophers who blur the boundaries between the human and other-than-human. They recognize that plants and fungi can potentially 'nurse' one another, and they question the 'motivation' of plants and fungi. They also wonder whether, in the face of danger, altruistic 'warnings' are given or whether opportunist 'eavesdropping' is undertaken. Whichever way one chooses to look at it, underfoot, the forest floor is a 'social' place where lives are 'orchestrated'.[3]

From a traditional vantage point – from where teleology does not embarrass, but instead enables empathy with nature – we could say that the forest floor is typically Sagittarian in showing concern for the well-being of both the individual or self and the community. It is a gathering of many hybrid identities or, maybe more accurately, one vast and ambiguous identity, a unified guild of life-forms, from the smallest invisible nitrogen-fixing bacteria, through the magnificent visible trees, to the enormous yet once again invisible fungal network.[4]

THE CONSTELLATION OF SAGITTARIUS is a centaur, armed with a bow and arrow. That arrow links the zodiac sign to November and December in the labours of the months, which sometimes featured hunters in a forest. Hunting requires keen sight, and the ability to hit a moving target from a distance requires a degree of foresight. The zodiac associates those born under this sign with the phrase 'I see'. But to 'see' has two distinct meanings according to the parable, 'because they seeing, see not; and hearing, hear not' (Matthew 13:13). Seeing can mean noticing the steam rising from a compost heap or the hoar frost-like saltpetre creeping across church walls and floors. It can also mean understanding the implications of what you see.

The human communities that enabled hunters to harpoon great whales to the brink of extinction, for example, evidently 'saw not', from an ecological perspective. On the other hand, after Leopold fixed a wolf in the sights of his rifle, squeezed the trigger and then looked into the wolf's dying eyes, his ability to 'see' was transformed from the prosaic to the profound. He saw the connection between an individual and the community of which they were part, and he understood the dire consequences of his action.

At a technical level, the everyday hunter's failure to 'see' the source of their power is part of Leopold's 'spiritual danger' of thinking that 'heat comes from the furnace'. In the Dog Days it was obvious that heat came from the Sun, but the hidden fire of cold late autumnal Sagittarius also originally came from the Sun. The power behind the arrow came from the Sun's energy, harvested by plant communities and stored in a bow made from the wood of a yew tree, and spun fibres from a field of flax, held together in tension. The (historic) bullet's power came from rich underground microbial communities, whose diet – on detrital pathways, fed by those who fell from grazing pathways and who, in turn, had been fed by the Sun – traditionally included the droppings of doves. Gunpowder explodes because, when charcoal, brimstone and the spirit of earth are touched by fire, they suddenly become air.[5] The hunter's ability to shoot a creature therefore comes directly from the communities in which both they and that creature are embedded, reinforcing how life and death are interwoven in nature.

Sagittarius shows slow fire's power to transform – purifying through putrefaction – and to destroy in order to renew. Modern science's exploration of the brown world's mycorrhizal networks is slowly starting to reveal the hidden webs of interdependency that sustain us, even through our darkest months when nature seems to have shut down. This is a time of exploration – seeing beyond surface appearances – and also of processing and sharing what will be necessary for the adventures that will unfold when light re-enters the world through the coming winter. It builds on last month's patience with a growing sense of anticipation, and it finds expression in the Christian tradition as Advent, the countdown to Christmas.

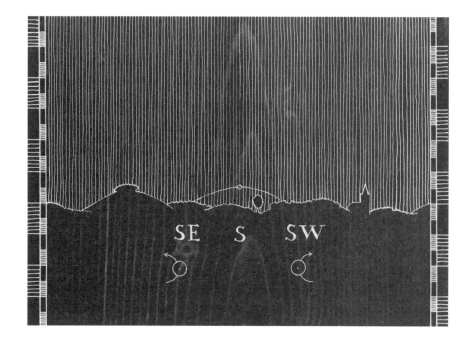

The Sun's path around the winter solstice at a latitude of 52 degrees north.

Winter Solstice

The winter solstice marks the end of the Sun's southbound journeys along the horizons.

In County Meath, Ireland, Sí an Bhrú or Newgrange is part of the Brú na Bóinne complex. Newgrange pre-dates Stonehenge and the Egyptian Pyramids and was built around 3200 BC by Neolithic farmers. It has a long underground passage that aligned with the winter solstice sunrise. Today, owing to a shift in the Earth's axial tilt, the alignment is no longer exact and, from about AD 5000, Newgrange's innermost chamber will be in permanent darkness until around AD 19000, when the oscillating Earth's tilt will return to its current angle.

In Irish folklore, Newgrange became associated with the father deity, Daghdha, his consort Bóinn and their son Aonghus. The fact that Newgrange contained the remains of the Neolithic dead and became the home of deities suggests a connection between the rising Sun and the idea of rebirth.[1]

The winter solstice – the shortest day of the year, around 21 December – marks the return of light in the world. In the Christian tradition it is marked, in time, by the birth of Christ and, in space, by the architectural tradition of orienting churches towards the east, facing the rising Sun.

Capricorn, based on star chart in Andreas Cellarius' *Harmonia Macrocosmica* (1661).

TEN

December–January
Cardinal Earth,
'Return of the Light'

lthough, psychologically, winter might seem to have started around Halloween, cosmically, Capricorn marks the actual start of winter. The earth looks bare but life has completed its retreat and, at last, the days are starting to grow again, even if imperceptibly at first. Leafless trees have turned their attention inward, readying themselves for the coming year's weight and responsibilities. Of course, evergreens like the yew are exceptions, but even they, along with the rest of the world, can be covered by a pure, unifying blanket of snow, frost and ice. That wintry covering resolves superficial differences and serenely brings everything together.

Capricorn is earth's first – cardinal – appearance in the zodiac. We saw fixed earth's beauty in Taurus and mutable earth's service in Virgo, but now, at the start of the (calendar) year, we experience earth's stillness. This still season immediately follows the solstice, when the Sun stood still, a point when that which is above met that which is below, when the Sun bent down towards the Earth. The season's stillness can also be enhanced by the mysterious calm that descends with a blanket of snow.

Since earth is the most immobile element and because all things contain the seed of their opposite, this month's stillness is, perhaps paradoxically, the source of the whole year's movement. And since the word 'cardinal' comes from the Latin for 'hinge', while January gets its name from Janus – the gods' janitor or doorkeeper – it could be said that this month is the stationary hinge that enables the door to open and close, bidding farewell to the old world while ushering in the new. This earthly stillness is also appropriate for a sign ruled by heaven's slowest planet, Saturn.[1] Stillness is a faint echo of eternity, the container of time, and time, of course, is the container of all events that happen under the sphere of the Moon.

FOR PLATO, THE element earth lay at the very centre of the geocentric universe and, while it was the principle of stability, it also reflected a greater Reality, like everything else in the Realm of Becoming. Elemental earth's immobility reflects the immutability of the Realm of Being and, mirroring that Realm, earth potentially contains all possibilities. Yet earth can only help bring life to all those possibilities after solid rock has been thoroughly divided. Only when completely broken down and actually indivisible can earth properly reflect heaven's immutability. Only when matter is fully decomposed can it be recomposed into new forms.

But of course, there are no universal laws under the sphere of the Moon. So, while life-forms can access mineral riches more easily when rocks are broken down, there are exceptions. Lichen, for example, seems to thrive on the solid rock of old tombstones. However, according to modern science, lichen is not a single life-form but an intimate embrace of two life-forms. Lichen is composed of algae, which provide sugars, and rock-digesting fungi, which provide minerals. It is a miniature version of a conjoined forest canopy and mycorrhizal system. Last month's mutable activities showed how life could access and redistribute mineral wealth, yet what is it about the lifeless that makes it able to offer itself to the living?

Beneath our feet, earth seems as solid as ever, yet, imperceptibly, it is being broken down, just as detrital pathways broke down fallen life-forms. All through winter, apparently lifeless water penetrates tiny cracks, turns to ice and expands to force the cracks open, a process that – in roads – rips apart tarmac to make potholes. In nature, this freeze–thaw cycle steadily gnaws away at solid rock, breaking down vast boulders and eventually turning them into ever-finer grit. Throughout winter, liquid water turns to solid ice and back again, over and over, until seemingly impregnable rock is opened up to accommodate life. Of course, glaciers, mountain streams and rivers also grind down solid rock to help give life a foothold, and they do it all year round. And where water does not generate freshly fragmented earth, air and fire do, the elements constantly cycling, as in the zodiac. For example, millions of tons of fertilizing wind-blown Saharan sand are deposited on the Amazon basin every year and, sporadically, volcanos spew fertilizing ash across the whole globe.

The apparently lifeless freeze–thaw destruction of rocks – and roads – is usually described as an inanimate process that involves materials which are usually called inorganic. Those terms come from nineteenth- and twentieth-century science, and they suggest that the materials and processes are physical, and so quite different from the biological materials and processes involved in the cycle of life. But this hard modern distinction – with things being either alive or dead – differs from traditional distinctions, which can see materials and processes as varying in their degrees of animation.

THE UNDERWORLD'S SLOW mineral rhythms and the geological changes that unfold through deep time are accommodated in mythological perspectives that embrace vast timescales, like the Hindu day of Brahma and Plato's Great Year. Within those cycles, everything is considered animate, a mixture of matter and spirit, and everything – even the most seemingly barren rock – houses some aspect of the spirit in matter. Different rocks derive their different characters from mixtures of forces, emerging from below as well as descending from above. Traditional cultures celebrate the celestial forces embodied in minerals, harnessing them in medicine and using them as supports for prayer. Faint echoes of those mineralized heavenly forces survive in today's concept of birthstones, each of which embodies the month's astral properties. For example, January's birthstone is garnet, and its name – from the Latin for 'seed' – acknowledges its animate nature. The way red garnets grow over their rocky matrix – from the Latin for 'womb' – looks like ever-fresh split pomegranate.[2]

Premodern cultures also recognized the potential danger of subterranean forces, so guarded against them with taboos and rituals, especially in activities like mining. The Egyptian word for mineshaft also meant uterus and, around the eighth century BC, the Greeks described rocks as being born, begotten and engendered. Long before Shakespeare wrote of saltpetre torn from Earth's 'bowels', in the first century AD, Pliny said that miners violated Mother Earth, probing her 'entrails' (*Natural History*, XXXIII). As heroes like Aeneas knew, venturing underground was perilous.

Around the same time, Ovid said that nature crafted grottos and shrines for divinities from 'living stone' (*Metamorphoses*, III). And, acknowledging those natural processes, the rusticated finish of classical-style building stones is meant to show that they are still rooted in Mother Earth and so still alive. Rocks could also be gendered, so, for example, flint could be either male or female and when pieces of flint that were sexually attracted to each other came together, sparks flew. Also, when red sard and white onyx mated, their offspring was red-and-white banded sardonyx, the favoured stone for cameos. Cameos artificially mimicked fossils, which were said to be images formed by natural forces that included emanations from the stars.[3]

MODERN SCIENCE IS now softening its distinction between the living and the non-living. Of course, it tends to reduce the living to the non-living and it does not express their connections poetically; none-theless, it does recognize important interchanges between the two realms. For example, the tar in tarmac is seen as a residue of the trees and animals that lived in forests that have long since fallen and been buried. No matter how alien the Underworld might seem to us, the difference between it and our world is only a difference of degree, not a difference of kind. In fact, things in the non-living world – like ostensibly inanimate rocks – can only support life because they have already had relationships with the living. Being mineral is a wintry period of repose in life's long and sometimes difficult journey. According to the Persian poet Rūmi, being mineral is an essential step in the return to God (*Mathnawī*, VI, 125).

Flint, for example, seems far removed from life. After all, for millennia, knapped-flint axes, knives and arrow-heads helped take life, as, for centuries, did pistol-flints. Yet, while modern science no longer considers flints to be alive or gendered, it does recognize that they have their origin in things that were indeed alive and gendered. Odd-shaped solid flint nodules – including 'hag stones' – were formed by fluid flint flowing into cavities made by creatures that burrowed through chalk. Those flint nodules are the casts of tunnels and the like, mineral traces of life's activity, like dinosaur footprints in fossilized mud. And the once-milk-like flint itself was the dissolved remains of creatures like sponges and microscopic diatoms that lived and died in ancient oceans and whose skeletons and shells settled on the sea floor.[4]

The porous chalk matrix through which the flint percolated, settling in holes made by plants and animals, also had its origins in life. Thick geological layers of chalk are the bodily remains of other, mainly microscopic, sea creatures whose shells settled on ocean floors over tens of millions of years. Modern science sees chalk as a natural form of calcium carbonate, and the carbon in the ancient sea creatures' shells itself came from many other life-forms. Those animals and plants released their carbon – as carbon dioxide – when they breathed out or were burned down. Exhalation or fire circulated their carbon in the air until it dissolved in water and made its way to the oceans, where it was used by sea creatures to help make their shells and – in some parts of the world – eventually become the earth upon which we walk.

When earth compresses and heats chalk, it turns into limestone and marble, and some of the shells in that chalk – then limestone or marble – are large enough to see. So, preserved seashells in those hard stones alerted the ancients to earth's animation, both its migration from ocean floors to mountain tops and its ultimate connection with life. That elemental circulation was not just evident to those who climbed mountains, because people celebrated it with polished marble floors. They even actively participated in that very same circulation of matter to make their buildings.

For example, lying beneath the soil of eastern England are many layers of soft white chalk, some of which contain hard black flint nodules, which are ideal for facing the walls of fishermen's cottages or parish churches. The chalk was transformed into lime mortar to fix the flint facings, while untreated chalk filled wall cavities. Lime mortar was produced by roasting chalk, which made it release the carbon dioxide that countless microscopic sea creatures had taken in millions of years ago. The lime was mixed with water, then laid between flints and, slowly, the mortar breathed in carbon dioxide from the air to turn back into solid chalk.[5] The carbon dioxide that the mortar breathed in came from the original chalk that had been roasted and from the burnt firewood, as well as from the breath of those who worked in the kilns, built the walls, lived in the cottages and prayed in the churches.

People took flints out of their original chalk matrix and embedded them in a new chalk matrix using a process that echoed nature's interactions between the mineral realm and the breath of life. Cottage and church walls of flint, chalk and mortar are part-artificial and part-natural. They are entwined inanimate–animate, earth–breath or matter–spirit composites while, biblically, humans are also an earth–breath composite (Genesis 2:7). It is therefore not so surprising that thick, solid church walls were no barrier to the saltpetre or 'spirit of the earth' that migrated from bodies buried in the graveyard to grow like hoar frost in the nave. In practice, the animate and the inanimate constantly interact, making it difficult to find meaningful distinctions between them. Modern science's hard distinctions – as well as its dismissal of taboos about releasing chthonic forces – have unleashed dangers like climate change.

While the carbon that is sometimes in seashells' calcium carbonate constantly circulates, so too does the calcium, although of course it moves through the world in different rhythms and along different pathways. Via grass and clover, and milk and cheese, we eventually use that same calcium to strengthen our bones and teeth. In fact, much more chalk or lime was spread across fields to feed plants and animals than was ever used in buildings. This ancient, and continuing, farming practice replenishes the soil with calcium and it echoes the ancient practices of miners who sealed up old mineshafts, enabling – according to Pliny – precious rocks and ores to replenish themselves (*Natural History*, XXXIV). Like obstetric surgeons, traditional farmers and miners took care to heal Mother Earth's postpartum wounds. And the iron in our own blood – which we use in the life-giving exchange of carbon dioxide and oxygen – also comes from minerals deep in the Earth where, thousands of millions of years ago, it had already been used by bacteria to help them breathe.[6]

THE ZODIAC ASSOCIATES THOSE born under this sign with the phrase 'I use'. The earth that supports us has been used many times before by many different creatures. Deep earth contains the remains of the ancient dead – in silicon-, calcium- and iron-based minerals

– and, closer to the surface, these are joined by the remains of more recent dead – buried, decomposing plants and animals – in humus. This month's zodiac sign is associated with using resources with ambition, or upward movement – from solid rock to fertile soil, from plants' roots to their leaves, from scavengers and herbivores to carnivores – all with an eye to continuing the cycle of life.

Of course, with such constant circulation of minerals, earth is not really still. It just seems so. Even though the days started to grow after the solstice, nights still dominate and life's growth is hidden, closed over by earth. That invisibility is like the first few days of the month when the Moon's initial growth is invisible – hidden by the light of the Sun – so we only see the new Moon when she is already a few days old. Even though nature works constantly in the Underworld, we must wait to see nature's radical work in our world.

John Clare said that, while it may be 'Trampled underfoot/ The daisy lives and strikes its little root/ Into the lap of time' (*The Eternity of Nature*). Plant roots – helped by fungi – channel most of life's minerals, growing down into the 'lap of time' to bring up gifts from our ancestors. Some of those gifts are from those who were once close to us, including cremation ashes and last year's leaf-mould, while others are from distant beings, geologically processed over aeons. Roots and detrital pathways engage with past life in order to promote future life so that what went before will produce what is yet to come. Life rises from the realms of the dead. Although Mother Earth seems to produce from herself, exactly how she does it we cannot know. The Underworld's mystery was expressed mythologically by taboos – such as Persephone being 'she who cannot be named' – and by traditions, including one that Hades had a helmet which made him invisible. Everything about the Underworld was unspoken and unseen.

NONETHELESS, WHILE UNSPOKEN and unseen, some aspects of the Underworld's mysteries were known and expressed in everyday life. One way that nature's hidden mysteries were expressed was in craft secrets, including how builders made lime mortar, echoing natural interactions between minerals and life-forces. Another Underworld-like hidden craft secret was how painters made their purest colour from materials and processes related to Capricorn.

Just as the fixed stars' cosmic influences were embedded in stones – like January's birthstone, garnet – the wandering planets' influences were implanted in metals, and Saturn, the planet that rules Capricorn, manifests its particular qualities in lead. Saturn is far from the Sun so is cold and has a long orbit, making it an ideal model for the Earth's slow wintry processes. And, if Saturn is an intelligent body in the heavens, then lead reflects its intelligence embodied on Earth. If, after the solstice, light gradually emerges through Capricorn's dark days, then light also gradually emerges from Saturn's dark metal, which materializes light as a pure white powder. This was one of the earliest synthetic pigments and artists made it by burying coils of lead under a heap of vinegar- and urine-soaked rotting manure. These coils were dug up a month later – recipes do not specify which month – and the growth of tiny crystals that covered them like snow was scraped off to make paint, medicine and cosmetics. In the dung heap, the by-products of life decomposed (like last month's fiery Sagittarius) to engender a slow change in a subterranean material (like this month's earthy Capricorn). Like lime mortar, it was an interaction between a mineral and a life-force, and it made the artists' favourite white for around three thousand years.

The vinegar- and urine-soaked rotting manure is an enhanced compost. The products and remains of recent life – and their combined heats of fermentation and metabolism – penetrate the lead, albeit in a gentler way than the lime-kiln's fire penetrated chalk.[7] The lead is thus joined with life or, in the terms of modern science, it becomes an 'organo-metallic complex'.[8] It then slowly breathes in carbon dioxide – just like the lime mortar – to form snow-white crystals of lead carbonate. The artists' process transforms a black, malleable metal into its opposite: a white, crumbly powder. And the process – burial under dung – seems like a ritual humiliation that reminds us of our own connection to the earth, since the word 'humiliation' shares its root with human and humus. (Of course, the earth also transforms both humble bird droppings and our own buried corpses into that other white crystal, saltpetre.) Putrefaction brings forth purity.

THE UNDERWORLD-LIKE TRANSFORMATION of black metal into white powder was a behaviour unique to lead. It was a craft secret, an aspect of Saturn best known by artists and alchemists. Everyone else knew Saturn as the god of time and agriculture. He was not the most popular of gods, not least because he was often depicted as a sad old man devouring his children. (Saturn was also linked – through cold, dry earth – to melancholy and, as all-devouring time, he ate his children, along with everything else.) But Saturn also presided over one of the most popular Roman festivals, Saturnalia, a week-long celebration in which gifts were exchanged, codes of behaviour loosened and roles reversed. This social role reversal – a world upside-down, with masters becoming servants and servants, masters – mirrored the Sun's reversal, descending then ascending around the solstice. Paradoxically, Saturnalia's revels marked the still point at which time can be escaped.

In the zodiac, the year's still hinge has the potential to reveal what Dante called the 'other way', which he said could take us to 'what is eternal' (*Inferno* 1, 91; *Paradiso* 31, 38).[9] Solstices symbolized the migration of souls, their birth and their death, their descent into earthly embodiment and their ascent from an earthly body. In particular, the winter solstice was the 'gateway of the gods' when heavenly beings came down to Earth (Porphyry, *On the Cave of the Nymphs*).

In the Christian tradition, the winter solstice and the emergence of light from darkness were marked by Christ's birth. It has been said that Christ's birthday usurped pagan festivals, including those dedicated to Saturn or Sol Invictus, which may be true. However, it is also true that a birthday at the winter solstice is fully in accord with Christ's earthly life-in-the-flesh. He was conceived at the spring equinox – to be mirrored by his death, also at the spring equinox – so, after nine months in Mary's womb, he would be born on the winter solstice, around 25 December in the Julian calendar.[10]

God said 'Let there be light' (Genesis 1:3) and 'Let light shine out of darkness' (2 Corinthians 4:6). As the Son of God, Christ was the 'true sun' (Malachi 4:2) and affirmed 'I am the light of the world' (John 8:12). That light's eternal nature is reflected in the Sun's periodic return at the beginning of every winter.

Aquarius, based on star chart in Andreas Cellarius' *Harmonia Macrocosmica* (1661).

ELEVEN

January–February
Fixed Air, 'Information'

Awarning is in order before we consider Aquarius. Or, being sensitive to the origins of the word 'consider', before we 'place our
minds with the stars of' Aquarius. The Preface acknowledged
that the zodiac and ecology might seem strange bed-fellows, although
the previous chapters have hopefully shown that both address some
of the same questions about nature, even if from different vantage
points. Now, this chapter will address an aspect of nature – hylomorphism – which is fundamental to traditional sciences but which
mainstream modern science does not recognize. (However, closely
related cosmological ideas still thrive and inspire radical thinking.[1])

Aquarius is winter's second sign but, uniquely in the annual cycle,
its ruling planet does not change. In fact, for the Romans, so little
seemed to change in early winter months that they didn't even bother
to count them until Julius Caesar added January and February as
'intercalary' months. His actions resynchronized the calendar with
the Sun but also turned September and October from the seventh and
eighth months – as their names suggest – into the ninth and tenth
calendar months.

Saturn's continued presence is consistent with its slow orbit and
its position, furthest from Earth and closest to the fixed stars. It is as
if, last month, the zodiac's orderly sequence of ruling planets was still
ascending the cosmic ladder but, having reached the top, it now
starts to descend. Last month's ascent accorded with the qualities of
time associated with building and ambition, of nature raising the

Underworld's minerals to the biosphere. This month's descent of the ladder is in accord with the equally necessary heavenly influences that must fall to complement those rising subterranean forces.

The balance of ascending chthonic influences and descending celestial influences reflects hylomorphism, one of the zodiac's guiding principles. Hylomorphism suggests that the whole universe – from stars, through people and earthworms, to stones – is made from mixtures of 'matter' and 'form', the Western equivalents of *yin* and *yang*. Form corresponds to *yang*, to the biblical upper waters and to the unchanging Platonic Archetypes in the Realm of Being. The zodiac acknowledges both the Realms of Being and Becoming so the relationships it represents straddle the atemporal and the temporal.

Hylomorphically, all things in our Realm of Becoming are constantly changing temporary unions of form and matter. The world we know is a regularly re-woven fabric of vertical warp threads (form) and horizontal wefts (matter). For example, as matter, calcium sometimes contributes to seashells, sometimes to chalk ground and sometimes to our bones. But wherever it finds itself, calcium's form is always the same: an arrangement of twenty protons, twenty neutrons and (in cationic form) eighteen electrons. Neither pure form nor pure matter exists. After all, in terms of traditional science, even modern science's atoms are mixtures of matter in some form. For example, carbon's matter also consists of protons, neutrons and electrons, while its form is six of each. Not even those sub-atomic particles are pure matter since they too have some kind of form, even if it's only mathematical.[2]

Things that seem close to non-existent pure matter or pure form – like sub-atomic particles and slime moulds (with apparently little form), or spirits and angels (with apparently little matter) – are mysterious. Saturn, however, is at home with both extremes of the form-and-matter spectrum. Saturn presided over the Underworld's mysterious (material) influences and now it presides over the heavens' even more mysterious (formal) influences.

AQUARIUS IS AN AIR SIGN, and the air is a subtle sea filled with invisible traffic. Our eyes, ears and noses are like harbours that receive immaterial and constantly changing lights, sounds and smells. The year's other air signs – mutable Gemini and cardinal Libra – involved connections between flowers and insects on the one hand, and between the worlds of light and darkness on the other. Both those signs involved horizontal, weft-like connections between things that change, like creatures and seasons. But now, fixed air acknowledges the vertical, warp-like, unchanging connections with the forms that the Realm of Being mysteriously gives the Realm of Becoming. (After all, calcium's form never changes, whether it's in a seashell, in chalk or in our bones.) And precisely because the heavens' formal contributions are mysterious, they are best approached indirectly, following the traditional practice of using the visible and material as guides to the invisible and the immaterial.

In the previous chapter we acknowledged that some of the matter in tarmac came from dead and buried trees and that, in time, it would contribute to trees that are yet to come. The connections between those once and future trees stretch across time and across the sea of air. For example, Shakespeare said that the spirit of air, Ariel, once spent twelve years imprisoned in a tree. It seems that Ariel had been breathed into 'a cloven pine' (presumably, in modern terms, as carbon dioxide) and then, after twelve years (in the form of starch or cellulose), he had been breathed – or burned – out again, free to wander among, and connect up, all four elements. Then, Ariel claimed to 'drink the air before me, and return/ Or ere your pulse twice beat'. He was also at home in fire, water and earth, 'when baked with frost'. Ariel fulfilled his tasks faithfully, under threat of being imprisoned in another tree – 'the knotty entrails' of an oak, this time – for a further twelve years. He acted at Prospero's bidding, under the influence of 'a most auspicious star' (*Tempest*, I, ii, and v, i). In traditional terms, Ariel's wanderings were material and horizontal while the star's guiding influence was formal and vertical.

Air also carries the matter that supports life in the form of smoke, scattered ashes and wind-blown earth. That matter is shape-shifting, and countless millions of tons of it float, unseen and seemingly weightless above our heads, in the porous borders between life-forms. These horizontal weft-like connections are acknowledged in the funereal 'Earth to earth, dust to dust, ashes to ashes'. Echoing last month's freeze–thaw fragmentation, such finely divided matter marks the end of one life and the beginning of another. Or, as the Bible puts it, 'Dust thou art and unto dust shalt thou return' and 'Thy seed shall be as the dust of the earth, and thou shalt spread abroad to the west and to the east' (Genesis 3:19 and 28:14). This airborne matter colours the sky. So, a dust-laden red sky is a heavenly reminder of mortality, which says to those who remain, 'I once was as you now are; you will be as I now am.' And modern science has shown that this reshuffling of matter – between the living and dead – is an ongoing process, suggesting that whatever our age, most of the cells in our bodies are only up to about ten years old.[3] Since most of our body's matter is constantly being recycled, the red sky can also say – twisting the words of the medieval *memento mori* – 'You once were as I now am; I will be as you now are.' The east is the direction of the rising Sun, spring and rebirth so, poetically, we could consider eastern red skies as a reservoir of matter from which we are, piece by piece, assembled. Similarly, since the West is the direction of the setting Sun, autumn and death, western red skies could be a reservoir to which we will, piece by piece, contribute. But of course, all past and future generations – of all creatures – mingle across the whole sky. Each living entity on Earth is a harbour that gives temporary berth to materials which have, at some time, flown through the air. And that restless airborne matter includes water.

Aquarius is the sign of the water-carrier, often depicted as a person pouring water from an earthenware pot. The air is a very efficient water-carrier but, unlike an earthenware pot, the sky has no sides. In fact, precisely because it has no sides, the sky is the world's biggest water-carrier, and now – owing to climate change – it's carrying more water. Much of it flows through invisible 'atmospheric rivers' about 2,000 kilometres (1,240 mi.) long and 400 kilometres (250 mi.) wide which, when they hit land, are now causing increasingly devastating floods.[4]

Water borne by the air came from trees, rivers and seas, and sometimes on winter mornings we can actually see it start its journey as mist rising gently above meadows, like steam over strangely still water. As morning mists dissolve, their water invisibly rises higher and higher until it condenses into tiny droplets that reflect the light, together becoming visible as white clouds. If those droplets collide, they grow bigger until they absorb light and the cloud gets darker. The darker the cloud, the bigger its drops and the more likely they are to fall as rain. Dark clouds are vast water-carriers and they fill rivers that flow to seas which, under the influence of Sun and wind, then surrender water back to the air. This never-ending hydrological cycle was recognized long ago: 'unto the place from whence the rivers come, thither they return again' (Ecclesiastes 1:7).

IN THE HYLOMORPHIC terms of traditional science, the cycle of water, the cycle of earth, dust and ashes, as well as the cycle of air itself, involve horizontal – weft – connections. Of course, in the Realm of Becoming, form and matter cannot be separated, but the more mysterious vertical – warp – connections involve mixtures that are richer in form than in matter.

Shakespeare wrote about clouds blocking the Sun and symbolizing, among other things, anxiety, betrayal, death and melancholy. They were also emblems of change, each being 'inconstant' (*Edward III*, II, i). For example, a cloud could take the form of a 'camel', 'weasel' or 'whale'

(*Hamlet*, III, ii). A cloud's form could also be 'dragonish' or 'A towered citadel, a pendant rock/ A forked mountain or blue promontory' and – using the imagery of water carried in air – Shakespeare said that clouds 'mock our eyes with air' till they become 'indistinct/ As water is in water' (*Antony and Cleopatra*, IV, xiv).

The forms of Shakespeare's clouds were products of the imagination, conjured by one who looked 'not with the eyes, but with the mind' (*A Midsummer Night's Dream*, I, i). The zodiac – including Aquarius as the all-encompassing aerial water-carrier – was made with the mind, not the eyes alone. And it was made from an accumulation of what some have called 'images made by chance', like cloud shapes. However, those natural images were pieced together with the heartfelt recognition that nothing happens by chance, that all things happen for a reason, whether that reason is astronomical, meteorological, biological, geological or psychological, and whether or not that reason is – or ever can be – known to us.

IN THE WINTER of 1856, inspired by the form of snow, rather than clouds, and noting vertical, rather than horizontal, connections, Henry David Thoreau wrote in his *Journal*, 'How full of the creative genius is the air in which [snowflakes] are generated! I should hardly admire more if real stars fell and lodged on my coat. Nature is full of genius, full of the divinity; so that not a snowflake escapes its fashioning hand.' Nature's 'genius', its 'fashioning hand', is the heavenly form that shapes earthly matter. It is what lets molecules of water know how to collect in freezing air, gathering around an invisible speck of airborne dust. Nestling together, molecules of water grow into hexagonal forms, just as – following a different form – hexagonal crystals of calcium carbonate gather around grains of sand to make pearls.

As snowflakes lazily float down and surround us, they are reminders that we live not so much *on* the earth as *in* the air, the most easily overlooked element. And snowflakes that lodge on a coat are also easily overlooked because they quickly melt. Not surprisingly, Saturn's cold influence is more enduring on the interface with the Underworld. There, on the surface of puddles, pools and rivers, ice crystals can grow in straight lines which, while inescapable in the urban world, are strangely elusive in the natural world. The slower the crystals grow, the straighter their lines. Yet as hoar frost – the word 'hoar' means old, alluding to white beards, as seen in many depictions of Saturn – ice crystals can also grow on bare trees, making miniature tree-like, or dendritic, structures. On windows, ice crystals grow into even more complex patterns, such as those that Jack Frost etches.

It does not take an imagination of Shakespearian proportions to see images of ferns, fronds or feathers in Jack Frost's crystals. They can appear less mineral and more vegetable, perhaps suggesting a life-force latent within the ice. In the premodern world, such patterns embedded in minerals could be caused by petrifying forces, like those of Medusa's head, which – according to Ovid – turned soft seaweed into hard coral (*Metamorphoses*, IV). However, the shapes of most life-forms in stone – what we would call fossils – were said to be caused by heavenly influences. Some of those heavenly influences promoted such extraordinary fertility that – according to Albertus Magnus – 'even in stones ... there is impressed upon the material the shape of a man or that of some other species ... either by painting, or by making it [cameo-like] partly or wholly in relief' (*Book of Minerals*, II, iii).

Those heavenly influences were transmitted down to the Earth via the stars, travelling vertically – as worldly sights, sounds and smells travel horizontally – through the invisible sea of air.[5] And, in the nineteenth century, Thoreau echoed Albertus Magnus' thirteenth-century ideas when he compared the snowflakes lodged on his coat to 'real stars' and credited their form to a 'creative genius' in air that was 'full of divinity'. If fossils are the enduring form of heavenly forces embodied in the dense, stable, solid element of earth, then Jack Frost's passing fern-like forms are caused by heavenly forces embedded in the dense, but fluid, element of water. They are ephemeral fossils, destined to melt under the Sun or sublime back into thin air.

WHILE MOST MODERN scientists do not recognize the traditional idea of heavenly forms acting on earthly matter, the idea of invisible and immaterial forms acting on visible and material matter continues to lie at the very heart of modern language and technology. For example, so-called in-form-ation technology rests upon the combination of invisible, immaterial software and visible, material hardware. And, to the extent that it thrives, modern science does so by keeping an open mind and acknowledging that – as Shakespeare said – 'There are more things in heaven and earth, Horatio,/ Than are dreamt of in your philosophy' (*Hamlet*, I, v). To remain healthy, all sciences must continually challenge and change their accepted 'philosophies', and contemporary research suggests that nineteenth- and twentieth-century science's dismissal of many traditional ideas now seems highly questionable.[6]

And of course, there is always more than one way of looking at anything. For example, Shakespeare's Ariel may indeed represent the spirit of connecting – and periodically transformed – air, yet tensions between Ariel and Prospero also represent a conflict in the soul, in particular between reason and imagination. These different interpretations of *The Tempest* are both valid because – unlike modern science – the traditional sciences see human nature as an integral part of wider nature, where each reflects the other. And, since reason does not exclusively regulate human nature, reason cannot encompass wider nature either. So, in addition to the rational faculty, the traditional sciences also recognize supra-rational and sub-rational faculties, the rational being concerned with questions of *how*, while the supra-rational and sub-rational are concerned with questions of *why*. In human nature, the supra- and sub-rational shape the motives for our actions – the noble and base, respectively – which are traditionally represented by the virtues and vices. In wider nature they are represented by some heavenly and chthonic forces.

Of course, the action of heaven on Earth is not exclusive to this month. Like the ever-present stars hidden by the light of the Sun, these invisible aspects of life's cycle are hidden by spring, summer and autumn's activities. Winter's stillness gives us opportunities to focus, and now is the time for contemplation and understanding. So, the forms of snowflakes tell crystallographers about the molecular structure of water while the forms of clouds tell meteorologists about weather and climate, as well as telling us whether or not it is likely to rain. The zodiac associates those born under this sign with the phrase 'I know'.

Between them, stern Saturn and bitter midwinter direct us along paths to self-knowledge. In addition to being the god of time and agriculture – which is the art and science of knowing the right time to sow or harvest – Saturn is more generally a strict teacher and the principle of organization. As such, natural forms – like clouds and snowflakes – demonstrate Saturn's genius as a rigorous organizer. Together with the bleak suffering that cold, hard Saturn's months can bring, the mysterious darkness of midwinter is recognized as a very profound source of knowledge and understanding. For example, when the semi-legendary Danish King Hrothgar introduced his discourse on the dangers of power, he said, 'I who am telling you/ Have wintered into wisdom' (*Beowulf*).[7]

IT IS SAID that some places, such as libraries, have an 'atmosphere' of learning and that ideas seem to be 'in the air'. This is the sense that forms are already present but only come to our attention when circumstances allow them to manifest themselves in matter. Timeless fern-like forms, for instance, can come into being as fleeting arabesques on car windscreens or as shade-loving plants, while – as Thoreau also noticed – branching forms can embed themselves in matter as rivulets through sand, as veins in leaves, and more. According to hylomorphism, ideas are perpetual while matter changes, so forms must be in the air 'before' matter can be informed, even when that matter is just the 'grey matter' hidden in our skulls.

Yet, because forms are hidden and mysterious, our imaginations clothe them in material things to make them more accessible. Shakespeare, for example, clothed the air's intangible connectivity in his flesh-and-blood character Ariel, and we now clothe the information at the heart of life in the shape of the double helix of DNA, a shape that no one has ever seen, or will ever see, but which we can all visualize. (DNA's shape may have stuck in our imaginations because it echoed some already culturally established forms. Two helical snakes coil around Mercury's caduceus and – still used as a symbol for medical services – one snake coils around the staff of Asclepius, the Greek god of healing.[8])

Having dug in and grounded itself last month in Capricorn, life now inhales and is informed in Aquarius. Capricorn was earthy – in terms of elemental qualities, cold and dry – while Aquarius is airy – hot and wet – so the two consecutive signs are another meeting of opposites. This winter pairing exactly mirrors the summer's meeting of opposite watery (cold and wet) Cancer and fiery (hot and dry) Leo. These particular conjunctions of opposites are generative and are followed by mutable signs which distribute whatever they have generated.[9] In the light half of the year, summer's obvious produce was distributed by young, quick Mercury whereas, in the dark half of the year, winter's more mysterious produce – the combination of form and matter that underlies all manifest reality – will be distributed by the older and more measured Jupiter.

This midwinter sign is midway between the darkest time of the year – the winter solstice – and the time of balance between light and dark – the spring equinox – which reminds us that this fixed sign has, at its heart, the increase of light. It marks the invisible gestation of a dazzling creative genius within a dark and receptive matter, which, as King Hrothgar said, is 'wintering into wisdom'. In the Christian tradition, this life-giving embedding of divine intelligence is enigmatically expressed: 'In the beginning was the Word, and the Word was with God, and the Word was God' (John 1:1). The Word is, ostensibly, only a vibration in air, and while the Word may ultimately bring light and clarity, it has its origin in dark, apophatic mystery.

Pisces, based on star chart in Andreas Cellarius' *Harmonia Macrocosmica* (1661).

TWELVE

February–March
Mutable Water, 'Ensoulment'

L ike the previous chapter, this chapter addresses another aspect of life – the soul – that modern science does not recognize. It does so with elemental water's final appearance in the zodiac. Cardinal water introduced summer while fixed water marked the heart of autumn, and now, mutable water makes winter's gifts available to the life that will emerge in the spring. Following its recent encounters with fire in Sagittarius, earth in Capricorn and air in Aquarius, water has morphed from tomb to womb. Four months ago, Scorpio's fixed water took life apart in the darkening Underworld and now, Pisces' mutable water brings together all the parts that will make up new life in our lightening world. Those parts include matter and form, like the minerals drawn up from the earth, acknowledged by Capricorn, and the genius plucked out of the air, acknowledged by Aquarius. They could not be more different. This chapter will therefore consider them separately.

Form and matter's fundamental differences are reflected in our lives since we both breathe in and out, both grow and age, and participate in both life's grazing and detrital food chains. Fundamental differences are also evident in how we can approach the Earth's everchanging relationship with the Sun. For example, we can divide the year from equinox to equinox, into the halves dominated by light or darkness, or from solstice to solstice, the halves of growing light or darkness. And, as noted in the Preface, the modern world further subdivided nature with pragmatic and poetic approaches, as represented by James Watt's condensing steam in a piston and William Wordsworth's wandering clouds in the sky.

But crucially, water dissolves differences. Ordinary water is the ultimate mutable substance. It is in continuous flux, nature's material image of the ever-flowing river of time. It has no shape, yet takes the shape of whatever carries it, and has no colour, yet takes the colour of whatever it carries. It also has no taste, yet depending on what it carries, it tastes bitter, sweet or salty.

In the zodiac, Pisces is ruled by Jupiter. Three months ago, approaching winter, Jupiter ruled Sagittarius – a masculine or active sign, fire – and then the planet's expansive influence was expressed outwardly, between different organisms like trees and fungi. Now, approaching spring, Jupiter rules again but this time in a feminine or receptive sign, water, and here its expansiveness is expressed inwardly, within each organism. Hints of that inward expansion show in the snowdrops that emerge from bulbs, which are, of course, little sub-terranean water-carriers. Now, on a much bigger scale, tree buds are gently swelling thanks to the flow of more hidden water. Throughout the year, trillions of tonnes of water will move up through plants. In fact, together plants drink about double the amount that flows through all the world's rivers.[1]

IT IS OBVIOUS that water can carry the earth's minerals because, in the kitchen, water leaves the uninvited chalk that appears in kettles and washing machines.[2] In nature, it carries rock away from mountains that are no longer guarded by wolves. Rivers naturally take minerals down to creatures in the sea, but how does water take minerals up to where plants need them, for example, to the swelling buds at the very top of a tree? The mechanisms that draw mineral-enriched water up-wards, away from the Underworld and towards the heavens, are still not fully understood by modern science, but much of what has been discovered was already suspected by an eighteenth-century clergyman, the Reverend Stephen Hales.

Trees are miracles of hydraulic architecture that can lift gallons of water a hundred feet and, if they're lucky, they can do it for a thousand years. From the outside it looks effortless, but what's actually happening inside depends on the coordination of many factors. In the summer, there were continuous columns of water running through interconnected vessels, the tree's xylem, all the way from the roots up to the leaves. When the leaves were out, the Sun's heat caused evaporation from the top of the water column as vapour diffused out of the leaves and into the air. The loss of water from the leaves created tension in the column, pulling water up through the xylem. Water's extraordinary cohesion transmitted that tension all the way down to the roots, and there, the pull encouraged more absorption of water from the tree's mycorrhizal partners and the soil. Crucially, every single water column avoided being broken by air bubbles – which could cause something like an embolism in the tree – because every single one of the tree's millions of xylem cells had been born, like human babies, pre-wetted by water.

A few trees, like willows, are starting to unfurl their leaves now, but most are still bare. So – after the sap has descended, the xylem vessels are no longer full of water and there are no leaves – what pulls the water up?

Over summer, xylem carried many gallons of water and dissolved minerals up the tree to feed the leaves as they grew, and xylem is accompanied by a similar network, phloem, which carried water and sugar down the tree. These high-volume vessels are like veins or arteries and, in order to get the flow started, xylem is connected to another, much smaller, set of vessels, which are like capillaries. Throughout the winter, the tiny amount of water in these much thinner vessels does not go underground to avoid freezing, but instead moves into the heart of the tree's trunk and limbs. As the late winter Sun gradually warms the tree, this water moves back out towards the bark and reconnects with the xylem. These much thinner threads of water act as a wick, helping pull water up from the roots, enabling it to reach the buds and provide the nutrients they need to transform into leaves, which will start the heavy lifting next month.[3]

The wicking, or capillarity, that pulls water up the xylem is the same phenomenon that pulled water deep into tiny cracks, driving the freeze–thaw cycle that disintegrated solid rock. In fact, in severe weather, when the cold penetrates deep into the trunk, the forest's wintry silence can be disturbed by what sound like gunshots as the water in those capillaries freezes and explosively breaks the tree's heartwood.

A PRAGMATIC ENGINEER like James Watt would doubtless have appreciated the way trees distribute earth-enriched water. (He would also have noted the power of constrained water's other change of phase.[4]) However, he would probably have had more difficulty with that other Piscean activity, mutable water's distribution of immaterial form. The way in which water can be imagined to carry hylomorphic form requires a poetic engagement with nature. But first, we need to step back and consider how things travel through time, starting with how they come into being in the first place.

While frost can inwardly deconstruct trees, it also outwardly re-constructs them, although hoar frost's tree-like forms are orderly arrays of molecules, whereas trees themselves are assemblages of cellular structures. When life descended into the mineral realm at the beginning of winter, we noted that the difference between the inanimate – like hoar frost – and the animate – like a tree – was a difference of degree, not of kind. And now, as life starts to ascend at the end of winter, it is appropriate to consider exactly how all animals, vegetables and minerals – whether cellular assemblages or molecular arrays – are formed.

TRADITIONALLY, all things come into being as a result of four causes, which are best illustrated with the way something like a crafted object comes into being. A chair, for example, has a *material* cause, which is the wood or metal-and-plastic from which it was made, and a *formal* cause, which is the design or shape of what it will become. These are like the two sides of hylomorphism acknowledged in Capricorn and Aquarius, respectively. But a chair also has an *efficient* cause, which could be the carpenter or joiner who shapes the wood. (It is significant that Jesus followed Joseph as a joiner, one who gave heavenly form to earthly matter (Mark 6:3 and Matthew 13:55).) The chair also has a *final* cause, which is the purpose it was intended to fulfil. In a hylomorphic and teleological world, all natural things – including trees and hoar frost – also have these four causes.

The material and formal causes often tell us something about the efficient and final causes. A chair, for example, can look as if it was hand-made or factory-made, and intended for a small child or an office-worker. Works of art also illustrate relationships between the four causes. Traditionally, a patron's wish to have a painting, for example, is the final cause. The artist is the efficient cause, and together, they come up with a detailed plan, or formal cause. The artist then selects the painting's material causes, which could be canvas and oil paint. The four causes are hierarchical, with the final cause at the top and material causes at the bottom.

The final and efficient causes – the patron and the painter – are active higher beings who travel through time. The material causes – the canvas and oil paint – are passive lower beings who also travel through time. (After all, if the painter chose to use a linen canvas and linseed oil, they could both have come from fields of flax harvested the previous year, with the canvas made from spun flax fibres and the oil made from pressed flax seeds.) The formal cause is the way in which the higher beings act upon the lower beings to make a particular thing at a particular time. In the natural world, the causes also flow downwards, but their relationship with time is different – the formal, efficient and final causes all act on the material cause together.[5] In the natural world, the final and formal causes of animals, vegetables and minerals are of course completely beyond our perception, which makes it appropriate for the zodiac to acknowledge them during the dark winter months, when nature's activities are hidden.

According to Aristotle, the bundled final, efficient and formal causes together constitute the immortal part of a being: their soul.[6] This means that the English phrase 'body and soul' denotes the whole person, their material as well as their formal, efficient and final causes. Aristotle said that humans had rational souls, souls that are capable of reason, albeit swayed by the sub-rational and supra-rational. But we are only different in degree – not in kind – from animals, which have sensitive souls that are capable of perceiving and responding to their surroundings. And animals are only different in degree from plants, which have nutritive souls, capable of making food and reproducing (*De Anima*, II). We could also go one step further down the Great Chain of Being to suggest that minerals have existential souls, which account for their varying qualities and properties. Following Rūmi, we could also say that, ascending the Great Chain of Being, the higher souls build upon the lower souls so that, for example, the human soul is existential, nutritive and sensitive as well as rational.

SO, ALL THINGS WITH BODIES also have souls, including hoar frost and trees. And all are bound together horizontally by their bodies – their weft-like exchanges of matter, over time – which is the focus of ecology. They are also bound together vertically by their souls, their formal, efficient and final causes. Traditionally, a being's soul determines the way in which it participates in its celestial or terrestrial realm, whether star or planet, human or animal, vegetable or mineral. So, in traditional medicine, for example, there are correspondences between the way seven planets act in the heavens and the way seven organs act in the body. The previous chapter acknowledged a kinship between lead and Saturn, for example, and that particular formal cause, type of soul or vertical kinship also includes our skeletal systems. Another connects the Moon, the metal silver and the mind.[7] Such warp-like connections form the basis for traditional symbolism. This is why the lion is always regal while the wolf inhabits a dark place in our imaginations, despite the fact that, in ecological terms, both are apex predators. (Of course, souls also connect horizontally, so mutually dependent wasps and figs might be considered soulmates.)

IF WE ACCEPT ARISTOTLE'S DESCRIPTION of the soul as the body's bundle of final, formal and efficient causes, then form is carried in the soul, and the soul is traditionally understood to be watery. As W. B. Yeats asked, 'What's water but the generated soul?' ('Coole Park and Ballylee'). Mutable water carries form – or Thoreau's 'genius', the cosmic idea – by wrapping it up with the reason behind the idea (its final cause) and the ways the idea will be employed (its efficient cause) by the ensouled being. Such souls, and their connections, are central to the traditional European sciences. Equivalent connections in other cultures are the basis for the remedies sought by ethnopharmacology, for example, and their loss in modern culture has freed us to drive great whales and pollinating insects to the edge of extinction. Souls represent, among other things, the mysterious aspect of beings, the parts that we cannot fully understand. So, when King Hrothgar said he 'wintered into wisdom', he did so by knowing and also by accepting that which he could not know. In other words, by believing. The zodiac associates those born under this sign with the phrase 'I believe'.

But to believe does not necessarily involve a lower burden of proof than to know. Of course, there are some things we believe, that – given enough time and effort – we might come to know, one way or another. This, after all, is precisely how modern science works, dreaming up hypotheses then seeking evidence to confirm or refute them. Yet there are other things – like love, beauty and the soul – that we can never know completely and where our only options are to believe or not believe. This was fully appreciated in the traditional sciences, and Aristotle thought that if anything in science could be understood, then that understanding depended on something that could not itself be understood by science (*Metaphysics* 1026a). In the early twentieth century a young mathematician, Kurt Gödel, reinforced this impassable limit to what is knowable with his theory of incompleteness, which proved that any system must contain truths that it cannot prove. This might seem to deny the possibility of objective truth but, in fact, Gödel interpreted it as evidence of the exact opposite. He was a Platonist who believed in pre-existing Truths to which we only have limited access.

Here in the Realm of Becoming, we can never completely know anything. For example, we can never know what tomorrow will bring, so, from day to day, we live supported by our beliefs. In the light half of the year, in the warmth, surrounded by nature's riches, our uncertainties faded into the background. Yet now, in the sixth month dominated by darkness, in the cold and when nature seems barren, psychological fatigue allows uncertainties to loom large. This is especially true for those whose last harvest was meagre, whose supplies are low and whose livestock are running out of fodder. For them, body and soul are sustained by a belief that nature's fertility will return, mythologically represented by Persephone's return from the Underworld. This is the last month dominated by darkness and, psychologically, it is said that 'the darkest hour is just before dawn', so snowdrops' arrival now lift the heart, offering hope, symbolizing the perils of life's return.

IN THE FIRST century before Christ, Virgil wrote a poem about agriculture and working the land. There, he recounted how Orpheus crossed the Styx, venturing into the Underworld to retrieve his wife, who had died from a snake bite. Hades agreed to the return of Orpheus' beloved Eurydice on condition that, while leading her through the Underworld, Orpheus did not turn round to look back. They had almost escaped when Orpheus, lacking belief – either in Eurydice's love or Hades' promise – turned to check she was still following. Her ghostly form was instantly whisked away and they were parted forever (*Georgics*, IV).

Pisces presages the year's emergence from darkness and is represented by two fish bound together by a cord, just as Orpheus and Eurydice were bound together by love. In legend, Pisces' two fish are either transformations of Venus and Cupid, or fish that helped Venus and Cupid when they were pursued by a monster. Either way – unlike Orpheus and Eurydice – bound together, the mother and son of love both escaped (Ovid, *Metamorphoses*, V, and *Fasti*, II). More generally, fish are symbols of fecundity and embody the power of the water in which they live. In the night sky, Pisces' two fish swim in different directions, which may suggest coming and going, the end of one cycle and the beginning of another. Just as two-faced Janus marked the start of the new year – as defined by the decrease of light turning into the increase of light – so the two fish mark the end of the old year, this time defined by the dominance of darkness turning into the dominance of light.

In a world where gods might seek the assistance of fish, or seek refuge in the form of fish – and where countless nymphs and mortals were transformed into animals and plants, including narcissi and heliotropes – ensouled nature has a magical or dream-like quality. So, in addition to keen observation and critical reasoning, everyday engagement with nature also offered room for imagination and empathy, the heart of poetry. This was recognized by those who read the *Georgics* and who, over the centuries, changed the poet's name from Vergilius to Virgil. They recognized his almost magical ability to seamlessly graft stories – like that of Orpheus and Eurydice – on to a work about labouring on the land and, according to some modern scholars, they changed his name to accord with *virga*, Latin for 'grafting stick' or 'magic wand'. Virgil himself also recognized the magic of grafting and included a fabulously productive grafted tree in the poem's second book. Some modern scholars have interpreted Virgil's spectacular grafted tree as a decadent sign of hubris, as a shameful unnatural act. Yet an alternative interpretation is suggested by St Paul's comparison of God to an olive-grower, capable of grafting the people of one book on to the people of another book (Romans 11:16–24). That would make grafting less of an unnatural act and more of an act that harnessed the transcendent supernatural that is reflected in each being's soul. Horticulturalists also recognized that, in the everyday orchard, those trees with formal kinship – apples and pears, plums and peaches, oranges and lemons – had an almost miraculous ability to bridge from stock to scion, water dissolving their differences.

No amount of detail about xylem, phloem, capillarity or arboreal healing processes could distract a poet from the magic of grafting. For poets, the skilled joinery of living wood was a mystery to be embraced and celebrated. And yet another mystery comes at the end of this month, the last month of the equinox-to-equinox year. In the natural world, the end of one month slips unnoticed into the beginning of the next, but time's journey is far from straightforward and, at some point in the calendar, time's cyclic qualities have to be acknowledged.

At Pisces' end, the scion of the new year will seamlessly graft itself on to the stock of the old year, like the serpent turning to bite its tail, an example of the Realm of Becoming offering precious glimpses of the Realm of Being.

Having weathered two months of Saturn's cold, slow and heavy influence, Jupiter has quickened nature and winter starts to stir from its death-like slumber. Plato felt that, on awakening, we should recall our dreams and distinguish between the true and the false ones (*Charmides* 173a). True dreams came through the Gates of Horn, and false ones through the Gates of Ivory (Homer, *Odyssey* 19). And this month, as John Clare wrote in 'February' of his *Shepherd's Calendar*, is when 'nature of the spring will dream'. Very shortly, spring will arrive and nature's dream will have come true.

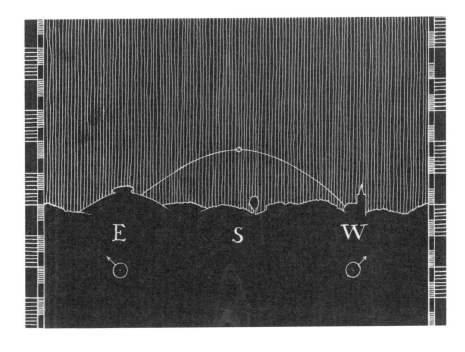

The Sun's path around the spring equinox at a latitude of 52 degrees north.

Spring Equinox

The spring equinox is around 21 March, when day and night are equal once again, but this time, day-length is increasing. The year turned the corner away from increasing darkness towards increasing light months ago, at the winter solstice. But it has taken time for the light to overcome darkness and it is only now, immediately after the spring equinox, that the light starts to dominate. Over the last three months, the Sun's heat has penetrated the Underworld's coldness, and life is now starting to revive. In the Christian tradition, the winter solstice's return of light was marked by Christ's birth. And now, around the spring equinox – when light eventually conquers darkness, or when life conquers death – is marked by Christ's resurrection.[1]

We have survived the harsh half-year of cold and darkness, and the return of light and warmth brings long-awaited relief. Around the spring equinox, the fruits of last year's labours start to show. Hidden seeds germinate and leaves unfurl, gradually greening barren land. The signs of decay fade away and everything seems fresh and new. We can look to the future with hope, welcoming new life and the bounty it promises.

We might make New Year resolutions around the winter solstice, but the spring equinox is when the natural world 'turns over a new leaf', again and again and again. Or, as Philip Larkin said, 'Begin afresh, afresh, afresh' (*The Trees*).[2]

Phaeton, based on the fictitious constellation on the ceiling of Villa Farnese in Caprarola (c.1575).

Next Year

E ven after turning over a new leaf, much of next year will most likely follow in last year's footsteps. The story of the year does not lend itself to a rip-roaring sequel because any particular year's story is like Chaucer's *Canterbury Tales*, a collection of stories within a story. Such 'frame stories' aim to imitate real life since neither frame stories nor real life have a single narrative arc and neither can be neatly contained within fixed beginnings and endings. In frame stories, as in real life, things always change and one thing leads to another, sometimes in ways we might expect and sometimes not.

It's probably safe to say that, next year, the qualities of time and rhythms of nature will be similar to last year's. We can expect life to assert itself and be enterprising and vigorous (as if saying 'I am'). Life will consolidate, being practical and secure ('I have'). Life will make connections and exchanges ('I think'). Life will nurture and be nurtured ('I feel'). Life will grow and exercise its power ('I will'). Life will serve, using method and reason ('I analyse'). Life will recognize diversity and encounter Otherness ('I balance'). Life will strive towards, and ultimately surrender to, one particular Other ('I desire'). Life will accept the Other through exploration and comprehension ('I see'). Transformed life will conserve and prepare itself with ambition ('I use'). That life will gain certainty with understanding ('I know'). And new life will be received with compassion and inspiration ('I believe'). All possibilities have their rightful time and, next year, if all possibilities are allowed their appropriate expression, life will go on. Life even continues through those difficult wintry periods that seem hopeless, fallow and barren.

Yet next year there will also be real differences, precisely because life on Earth supports so many possibilities. So, another twelve chapters could be written about the unfolding of time's qualities and they could be illustrated with stories about completely different animals, vegetables and minerals and their relationships. But time's unfolding qualities – as set by the heavens – are themselves also subject to change. Among the measurable changes is the shift of solstices and equinoxes through the zodiac signs that Hipparchus noted over 2,000 years ago. Of course, none of us will notice that three-day shift in the seasons every two hundred years. It's about one day in three-score-years-and-ten and it's completely lost in the weather's normal unpredictability. However, that particular difference is accompanied by other cosmic events, some of which we can see and some of which, historically, have helped people frame changes from year to year and generation to generation. One of them involves the orbits of Jupiter and Saturn, the two slowest-moving of the visible planets.

Jupiter's orbit is about twelve years and Saturn's is nearly thirty years, meaning that Jupiter regularly appears to lap Saturn. So, about every twenty years, Jupiter and Saturn meet in the same part of the sky, slowly coming together then drifting apart again. Over two hundred years, they meet ten times in parts of the sky – zodiac signs – that are governed by the same element, whether fire, earth, air or water. After that, they meet ten times in signs of a second element, then in the third, then the fourth until, after about eight hundred years, they meet back in signs of the first element again. In the zodiac, Jupiter and Saturn govern momentous changes and most of their twenty-year meetings are called 'great conjunctions'. Their once-in-two-hundred-years meetings, at the start of meeting in a new element, are called 'greater conjunctions'. And their once-in-eight-hundred-years meetings, after completing the cycle of four elements, are called 'greatest conjunctions'. The regularity of these meetings enabled cultures to mark distant events and chart slow changes. So, for example, a 'greatest conjunction' – when Jupiter and Saturn switched from meeting in water to meeting in fire – occurred during the life of Christ, then in the life of Charlemagne and again at the end of the sixteenth century.[1] That last time, it provoked some sensationalists to predict the end of the world which, when it failed to materialize, prompted widespread mockery.

Recently, Jupiter and Saturn met for the first time in an air sign – a greater conjunction – after about two hundred years of meeting in earth signs. But now, in the twenty-first century, most of us no longer worry about the astrologers' great, greater or greatest conjunctions or their fiery, earthy, airy or watery zodiac signs. Instead, we have our own, rather different, experts and we might worry about their technical concepts, like biodiversity, carbon footprints and global warming. However, just like the sixteenth century, we also have those who believe experts' predictions and those who choose not to.

The past two hundred years – when Jupiter and Saturn were meeting in earth signs – saw the study of nature transform into a modern science in which concepts like earthy or airy zodiac signs have been banished from respectable conversation. Recently, it has also become recognized that, over those same two hundred years, the products of modern science have had a significant impact on the balance of nature. So, in addition to natural changes – like the slow precession of the equinoxes – we are now beginning to see changes in the rhythms of the year caused by significant human disruption of the natural order. Some of those changes are now big enough and fast enough for us to witness over our own lifetimes. Sadly, the seasons that we experience now are no longer the seasons of our childhoods. And we are not simply the naive victims of nostalgia, because our lived experiences are reinforced by accounts of historic experience, like Gilbert White of Selborne's confident predictions about the return of migratory birds. As their nesting sites are destroyed and pesticides decimate their food supplies, it is now open to question whether swallows will be followed by martins then by swifts.

JUST AS OUR past determined our present, so our present will determine our future. The Preface noted that – as natural philosophy turned into modern science – the concept of nature was split in two. We could either engage with it romantically, as suggested by Wordsworth's appreciation of a cloud in the sky, or rationally, as in Watt's appreciation of steam in a piston. The impact of the imagination can be minimal, or it can be utterly momentous and world-changing. On the other hand, the impact of technology is incremental and, in the last two hundred years, technology's effects have been steadily transforming the human as well as the natural worlds.

Technology builds upon itself and, over about two hundred years, Watt's rather frail-looking steam engine had turned into the machines that O. Winston Link captured so dramatically in his *The Last Steam Railroad in America*. They had become heroic monsters that dwarfed the humans who tended them and dominated the communities through which they sped. Step by step, such monsters spawned others and, together, technological products – large and small – now seem to shape our lives more than nature. So, from day to day, technology may appear more powerful than nature. But, in the face of the raw elements, in the aftermath of wars and so-called acts of God – natural disasters and, in the wake of climate change, now not-so-natural disasters – technologies are still dwarfed by nature. In hurricanes, flash floods and forest fires, nature seems to have its own monstrous side.

Of course, nature's monsters have always been there, personified by the gods of wind, water and fire, as well as the dragons who guarded subterranean treasures and angels who guarded paradise.[2] But these mythical guards were not like today's nightclub bouncers who are only employed after the venue opens. Crucially, these mythical guards were the venue's joint architects. Monsters – like now-largely extinct megafauna, including mammoths and sabre-toothed tigers – were the integral guarantors of paradise, just as Leopold's comparatively modest wolf was the mountain's guarantor. In mythical terms, without dragons, there would have been no treasure to guard.

It is therefore not inconceivable that myths about the classical land of milk and honey or the biblical Eden may have some basis in historical truth. After all, to use just one example, once we have over-fished, dammed or polluted rivers, salmon can no longer reach their ancestral homelands and their populations plummet. Those fish that do survive shrink, and most no longer sacrifice themselves to feed the soil around their birthplace. Consequently, earthbound plants and animals that have no obvious connection with river- and sea-salmon also suffer and decline.

Year by year, historical records paint very clear pictures of ecological change that suggests a continued Fall from Paradise. For example, in mid-nineteenth-century Astoria, Oregon, there were salmon runs two hundred days every year, and fish weighing well over 100 pounds (45 kg) were common. Now, after extensive efforts to recover from historic population crashes, salmon numbers and weights are still significantly down. And, on the other side of the world, British government reports into North Sea fishing that date back to 1889 also suggest decline, which hardly seems surprising. However, when the increased efforts that now go into catching fish – more ships, more powerful engines, bigger nets, sonar and so on – were factored into the figures, the population decline was found to be not nearly 40 per cent but over 90 per cent.[3] Of course, North Sea fishing did not start in 1889 and the fish populations at the beginning of the survey were already significantly depleted. There are few reliable statistics further back but, in the seventeenth century, shoals of North Sea herring were said to be so vast that the sunlight which was reflected off their glistening backs illuminated the underside of clouds, enabling fishermen to hunt them from over the horizon. Tragically, the same story of lost riches could be told again and again, and from many parts of the world. For example, the author and marine biologist John Steinbeck celebrated life in 1930s Monterey, but the canneries of *Cannery Row* are now closed because there are no sardines left in the sea.

Of course, fishermen are allegedly prone to exaggeration, so today some people may have more faith in the accounts of historic naturalists like the Reverend Gilbert White. Yet his stories also suggest a lost past plenitude. In 1769, he mentioned a single tree that contained eighty herons' nests.[4] An English tree full of herons and coastal clouds underlit by herrings are unthinkable today. In a few hundred years, a relative paradise has indeed been destroyed. Such records of our decimation of nature are stark warnings, like the multilayered lessons – personal, social, political and mystical – that Ibn Khaldûn saw in the ruins of ancient, as well as not-so-ancient, civilizations (*Muqaddima*).

The actions of the last few centuries have caught up with us and humanity is now at a pivotal point. As the planet's top predator, we are also the creature most vulnerable to ecological change. After all, the kings of the North Pacific, orca, once enjoyed vast communal feasts on the occasional great whale, but we have now reduced them to relentless searches for slim pickings. The difference between us and other apex predators like the orca is that they are the victims of our behaviour, whereas we – for better or for worse – are, and will be, the authors of our own fate.

OVERFISHING, FARMING, HUNTING, habitat destruction and pesticides have already caused many extinctions but, in addition to ecosystems already weakened by diminished biodiversity, climate change now poses yet more threats. However, this is not the first time the climate has changed. It's changed many times before, sometimes slowly and sometimes quickly. Very slowly, ancient microscopic organisms that breathed with iron filled the air with oxygen. At the time, oxygen was a toxic waste gas and it drove an enormous number of species to extinction, but the change in the atmosphere's chemical composition slowly enabled new life – life as we know it – to emerge. On the other hand, very quickly, a prehistoric meteorite strike filled the air with dust, causing an 'eternal winter' that lasted for millennia and proved the last straw for dinosaurs.

Meteor strikes, eternal winters and dinosaur extinctions sound much more dramatic than today's imperceptibly increasing levels of carbon dioxide in the atmosphere. Yet science knows what effect carbon dioxide can have. Once upon a time, when it increased before, the effect was far worse than a meteor impact. About 250 million years ago – long after the iron-breathing bugs put oxygen into the air but long before the first dinosaur was even born – the level of carbon dioxide increased, probably because of volcanic activity.[5] It killed 96 per cent of all marine life.[6] Scientists call it the 'Great Dying'.

The effects of our own anthropogenic increase in carbon dioxide levels are happening much slower than a catastrophic meteorite strike but much, much faster than the effect of iron-breathing bugs. In fact, according to scientists, climate zones are now moving north through Europe at a speed of about 20 kilometres (12 mi.) a year. If it continues, this will mean that, in thirty years' time, London will have the climate that Barcelona has now. So far, nature's responses have varied, and insect-pollinated plants are responding more quickly than wind-pollinated ones, while, among trees, oaks are responding faster than ash, for example.[7]

Ecologists have been extraordinarily successful in demonstrating the almost unimaginably complex mutual interdependence of all things on Earth, whether alive or dead. And they have done so almost against the odds since ecology is a modern science, an activity that gained its strength by retreating from the messy real world into the clean, controlled laboratory and by disinterestedly studying selected parts of the world one at a time. But the picture that ecology has created still falls far short of establishing the unity of nature because – following Darwin's example – it excludes human nature. Modern science has successfully identified some fundamental changes to the natural world that have been caused by humans, but it is not particularly well equipped to address those changes. No matter how powerful modern science may have become, any method of exploration that systematically excludes human nature is at a disadvantage when it comes to considering how humans impact the natural world.

TODAY'S PREDICTIONS ABOUT the future of our climate all flow from the type of logical engagement with nature that the engineer Watt used to make his steam engine. Yet the poet Wordsworth's very different path, the path of the imagination, can also be prescient. For example, the 1982 film *Blade Runner* was a work of the imagination set in a fictional 2019, and it plays on dystopian anxieties about artificial intelligence and identity that are only now starting to surface as I sit at my kitchen table and write. The film was based on the book *Do Androids Dream of Electric Sheep?* which Philip K. Dick wrote in 1968, more than fifty years ago. But works of imagination can speak to us over centuries and millennia, as well as over decades. And, as well as having prescience, they can also have consequence.

One example of a work of imagination with consequence is a story about the spread of Buddhist scriptures. In the sixteenth century Wu Cheng'en wrote a mythic account of Tripitaka's real-world seventh-century pilgrimage (*The Journey to the West*). In the 1970s, every weekly episode of the story's TV version started by claiming, 'With our thoughts, we make our world' (*Monkey*). That profound truth is still recognized by those overcoming self-destructive behaviours like gambling or substance abuse. In the natural world of the Anthropocene, resource depletion, biodiversity loss and climate change are merely symptoms of our abusive and exploitative – and ultimately self-destructive – attitudes towards nature. The problems we have created need technical fixes, but technical fixes are not enough. The real solution has to include attitude changes.

Traditional mythologies can offer ways of overcoming our addiction to fossil fuels, for example, precisely because mythical ways of thinking about the world differ from modern scientific ways of thinking about the world. 'With our thoughts, we make our world.'

The preceding twelve chapters have tried to suggest that the zodiac can hold up a mirror to our relationships with the world. For millennia, frameworks like the zodiac helped people to see natural phenomena as role models. So, for example, our relationships with other humans and the natural world can be like Aries' maple or daffodil, like Taurus' daisy or ivy, or like Gemini's ant or bee. They can also be like the summer's wasps or figs, salmon or orca, seeds or earthworms. And they can be like autumn's winds or spiders, leaves or berries, fungi or saltpetre, and winter's flint or chalk, clouds or snowflakes, hoar frost or dormant trees.

Of course, winter's bare trees become summer's leafy arbours, so the zodiac also provides frameworks for understanding how our relationships with other humans and the natural world can change over time. Our relationships can change with the Moon's cycle, like vertically migrating plankton, or with the Sun's cycle, like the arrival of newborn lambs, or even approach Jupiter and Saturn's twenty-year cycle of conjunctions, like the seventeen-year cycle of some periodic cicada. The reach of European cultural astronomy is not as great as Indian cultural astronomy's, which – being sidereal – stretches much further back. Its range could encompass the rise and fall of entire civilizations and the passing of geological eras, including the Paleoproterozoic with its iron-breathing bugs and the Cretaceous with its calcium carbonate-shelled micro-organisms.[8] Mythically, the zodiac reminds us of our biological and historical relationships with all life on Earth. And, when so reminded, with different thoughts, we can make different worlds.

Recalling that the Potawatomi addressed maple reverentially as Maple, our thinking could shift away from a simply utilitarian idea of 'nature' towards the more respectful idea of 'Nature'. We could follow Thoreau, who knew that his local pond's waters 'mingled with the sacred water of the Ganges' and wrote about 'Nature' with a capital N (*Walden*, 'The Pond in Winter'). We can still recall that the lion is a king and that bees have queens, but we have largely forgotten – or, more accurately, over the last few centuries, we have radically cut ourselves off from – the roots of our own Western worldview. Meanwhile, recently, Indigenous worldviews have started to inform some successful moves towards environmental protection. And some of those moves have involved granting endangered natural phenomena the legal status of personhood.[9]

If Nature as a whole is a person, then, in the Western tradition, she is female. After all, etymologically, the Earth's matter is the mother, matrix or womb in which everything, including minerals, is engendered. Earthly Nature is the male sky god's fecund consort.

More than 2,000 years ago – reinforcing the roots of the Western worldview – Ovid also granted personhood to particular plants and animals, with stories about Narcissus, Arachne and others. He also wrote that the gods divided the globe into five climate zones, respectfully following the pattern of the heavens. There was a hot, equatorial zone, two cold, polar zones and two intermediate, temperate zones (*Metamorphoses*, I). He also told of a time when the climate changed and the poles heated up, when 'mountains lost their snow', 'rivers dried up', 'forests blazed', 'crops withered' and 'cities perished'. Ovid said these calamities were caused by Phaeton, son of Phoebus the Sun god, who – against his father's advice – borrowed Phoebus' chariot and horses to pull the Sun across the sky. Needless to say, the young Phaeton lost control and accidentally scorched both heaven and Earth before he crashed and burned (*Metamorphoses*, II). That particular climate change event was ostensibly the result of a single fateful day, but we should not forget that, in mythology, a day is not necessarily

24 hours. After all, in the Christian tradition, God made the universe in six days and, in the Hindu tradition, a day of Brahma lasts billions of years.[10]

Ovid also mentioned another mythical episode when 'crops perished' owing to 'too much sun or too much rain', which again sounds similar to the effects of today's climate change. That particular calamity was caused when Hades abducted Persephone, and it was resolved by Zeus who diplomatically divided the 'circling year' into 'two equal parts', enabling Persephone to 'share her divinity with two realms' (*Metamorphoses*, v). (As an aside, we could wonder whether Persephone's abduction and her subsequent alternation between our realm and the Underworld might mark the transition from the ancient Greek Age of Gold, with its 'eternal spring', to the Age of Silver, with its introduction of the other three seasons.)

Of course, at first sight, these mythic stories of crops withering and perishing seem to offer nothing to modern science's understanding of our own climate change. Initially, levels of atmospheric carbon dioxide – measured in hundreds of parts per million – seem completely unrelated to either Phaeton or Persephone. Yet when raised carbon dioxide levels are recognized to be the result of social relations between humans and other-than-humans, they are directly related to both Phaeton and Persephone. Like Phaeton's downfall, our own potentially catastrophic climate change is caused by hubris, the idea that we can alter the course of Nature with impunity. And the way we have altered Nature's course is directly linked to Persephone's 'two realms', and the delicate balance between our world and the Underworld. Ignoring that mythically negotiated balance, we have taken what was underground – coal, oil and gas – and put it into the air that we breathe. We have taken what rightfully belongs in the realm of the dead and raised it to the realm of the living.

A science that dismisses the poetic and the mythic might overlook these connections. But raising the dead can have its risks, as zombie movies make clear.[11] Zombie movies are part of a modern style of storytelling which is quite different from Ovid's storytelling, but all stories cater to the same basic audience needs and stories can transmit powerful ideas. It might even be that the most fanciful stories are the most memorable ones and, therefore, when faithfully interpreted, the most effective at transmitting hard-won knowledge.[12]

Ancient myths – like those embedded in the zodiac – represent all aspects of the real world, not just its physical aspects. They are all-inclusive because the traditional sciences upon which they are based embrace the whole of Nature, including human nature. They acknowledge Nature's Personhood so they can accommodate relationships – including the possibility of empathy – between the human and the other-than-human.

SO, WHAT WILL next year bring? Last year saw four seasons. First came spring, when light dominated and days were growing. Then came summer, when light still dominated but days began to shrink. Autumn followed, when days continued to shrink and darkness dominated. Then winter completed the cycle, with darkness still dominating but days starting to grow again. Nature and life responded to this rhythm of light and dark with springtime's hope, summertime's ease, autumn's contentment or trepidation – confidence or fear, depending on whether or not harvests had been good – followed by winter's hardship.

Spring brought warming, summer brought heat, autumn brought cooling and winter brought cold. Next year will also see four seasons, and next year's summer will certainly be hotter than next year's winter. But whether or not next year's summer and winter will both be hotter than last year's summer and winter will depend on collective action – whether we break our addiction to fossil fuels, for example.[13] Wu Cheng'en said that seasons pass 'like a weaver's shuttle' and, unlike warp threads, weft threads change (*The Monkey and the Monk*).

There are also equally important and much more deeply personal responses to the year's cycle of changes; all of us participate in Nature's repeated rhythm of hope, ease, contentment-or-trepidation, and hardship. Nature's example in springtime will always encourage hope in us. In fact, it is said that 'hope springs eternal', a phrase which might suggest that a glimmer of the mythical Golden Age – before Hades abducted Persephone? – endures in this Age of Iron.

But what of the qualities associated with the other seasons? For each of us there will be mixtures of hardship and ease, as well as mixtures of contentment and trepidation. The future's balance of hardship or ease will be determined by societies' collective actions and, one day, climate change may even reverse life's response to the seasons' rhythms. In the future, in some places, once-harsh winters may, in time, bring ease to the hardships of once-easy summers. However, the zodiac teaches that – whatever may have been sown and whatever will be reaped, whatever the balance of future hardship and ease – our balance of future contentment and trepidation is, to a greater or lesser extent, up to us.

Contentment and trepidation can be personal choices. And our potential power to choose comes directly from the traditional structure of realities, as described by the zodiac. As was said in the Preface, in our world – the Realm of Becoming – all changes are informed by the Realm of Being and happen because everything (human, animal, vegetable, mineral and elemental) participates (in both harmony and conflict) in an enigmatic journey from imperfection to perfection. Our emotional freedom to respond to the world comes from our catching glimpses of Being through the veil of Becoming. It comes as an automatic side-effect of the liberating vision that sees unity in diversity. This is the vision that William Wordsworth alluded to in the first version of *The Prelude*:

Tumult and peace, the darkness and the light
Were all like workings of one mind, the features

Of the same face, blossoms upon one tree,
Characters of the great Apocalypse,
The types and symbols of Eternity,
Of first and last, and midst, and without end.
(Book VI)

Living in such a world, our options of experiencing either contentment or trepidation can be guided by the zodiac because, unlike modern science, the traditional science from which it grew did not dismiss the poetic and the mythical. The zodiac is therefore better placed than modern science to recognize connections between human nature and wider Nature. It acknowledges the hubris that drove Phaeton and the passions that seized Persephone. It sees all-too-human arrogance and acquisitiveness as real factors with real consequences for the wider world. Those consequences may sometimes be unforeseen and unintended but they flow, inevitably, from the false modern assumption that humans are somehow separate from Nature.

THE ZODIAC IS an extraordinarily rich example of what Frances Yates called a 'memory theatre' (*The Art of Memory*). As such, the zodiac is not unlike its more familiar pale modern offspring, the everyday calendar.[14] Of course, its scope is much broader and deeper, because, while being a mnemonic structure that helps us connect events across time, the zodiac also engages with time in ways that can open up to the timeless. And, from the ways it interprets Nature and life in their swirling and sometimes overwhelming complexity, the zodiac has the potential to guide us. It helps direct us through the Realm of Becoming – the world of changing, and sometimes deceptive, appearances – towards the Realm of Being – Plato's constant, unchanging world of essences.[15] As the 'circle of little animals', the zodiac is profoundly embedded in an understanding of Nature that includes – in addition to animals – vegetables and minerals, the elements, the year, seasons and months, as well as human nature. And, when that vast, dazzling and dark array is seen through the zodiac's lens, we can use any aspect of it to help change our balance of contentment and trepidation. After all, as William Blake wrote, 'Joy & Woe are woven fine/ A Clothing for the soul divine' (*Auguries of Innocence*).

WE HAVE CONSIDERED how the seasons of the year have been perceived over millennia and, for next year's seasons to remain similar to last year's, we must minimize our impact on Nature. That, in turn, will minimize Nature's potentially wrathful impact on us. Yet, whatever Nature has in store for us, we can find peace with her by – to paraphrase Plato – seeking to align our own 'variable revolutions' with the 'unvarying revolutions' of the stars.

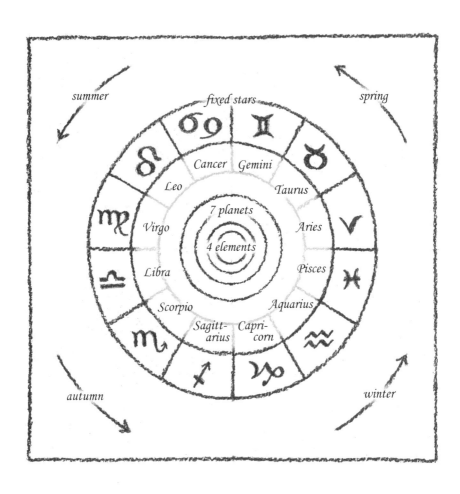

The zodiac.

The seasons referred to in this glossary are those of the northern hemisphere.

Air (see also Elements)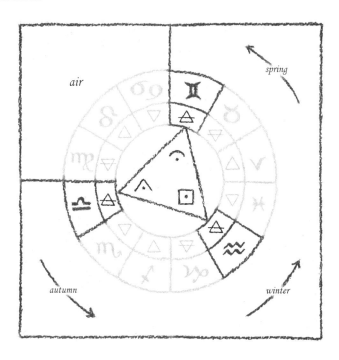

Elemental air is the subtle fluid, the connecting medium within which relationships are developed and enveloped. It is a masculine element, the combination of heat and moisture. Air introduced autumn in Libra, was at the heart of winter in Aquarius, and bid farewell to spring in Gemini. Then, having set the scene, it played no further part in summer.

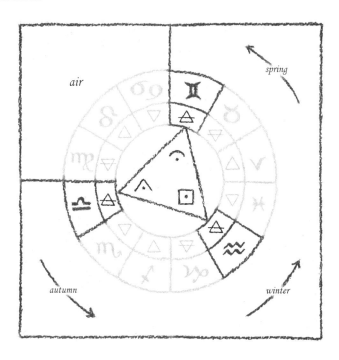

Autumn (see also Seasons)

Autumn comes into being with air in Libra, has water at its heart in Scorpio and passes away with fire in Sagittarius. Its rulers – Venus, Mars and Jupiter, respectively – are moving progressively further from Earth. Autumn is when the dark dominates and darkness continues to increase.

Cardinal (see also Fixed, Mutable, Seasons) /·\

The cardinal signs – Aries (fire), Cancer (water), Libra (air) and Capricorn (earth) – occur at the start of a season, immediately following a solstice or equinox. Cardinal fire (Aries) marks the beginning of spring, cardinal water (Cancer) the beginning of summer, cardinal air (Libra) of autumn and cardinal earth (Capricorn) of winter.

The cardinal signs form a cross – with two opposed masculine signs, Aries and Libra, and two opposed feminine signs, Cancer and Capricorn – dividing the year in four. The masculine members of that cross separate the half of the year dominated by light (from Aries to Virgo) from the half dominated by darkness (Libra to Pisces). The feminine members of the cross separate the half of the year when light increases (from Capricorn to Gemini) from the half when darkness increases (Cancer to Sagittarius).

Cardinal signs that follow the equinoxes (Aries and Libra) mark changes between the dominance of light or dark. Those that follow solstices (Cancer and Capricorn) mark changes in the increase or decrease of light or dark. Following the equinox and solstice's new relationships with light and dark, the cardinal signs all open up new paths, offering new directions through the world.

Dance

The Greek for dance was *horos*, which is the root of the words 'hour', 'horoscope' and 'horizon', the encircling boundary. Nature's circular dance consists of intricate exchanges between creation, preservation and destruction. In Nature, the dance is eternal but its interlocked rhythms and participants change. In Hindu mythology, the three dancers are Brahma, Vishnu and Shiva, and their trace could be said to weave a plait through time, like ribbons round a (European) maypole. In Greek mythology, the patterns of life's ribbons or threads were determined by three women, the Moirai. Clotho the creator spun the threads, Lachesis the preserver guided the threads and Atropos the destroyer cut them. They determined the fate of all things, including the fates of the gods. They made some of last year's individuals continue their dance, some to complete their turn, and others to enter the dance. In Nordic mythology, the dispensers of fate were the Norns (meaning 'to twine') and – through the Old English for 'fate', *wyrd* – they became the weird sisters, the wayward sisters and the three (wandering) witches.

These women's slow disappearance from our culture has cut us off from birth, life and death's cosmic pattern. However, the zodiac encoded their fateful wisdom. The zodiac is therefore able to teach lessons from Nature that are much, much more profound than those learned by Robert the Bruce, who was inspired by a persistent spider, or Tamerlane, Tamür the Lame, who was inspired by an industrious crippled ant.

Nature's elemental dance has four movements, the first of which is spring. In the first three steps, masculine fire's initiative is consolidated by feminine earth, whose progeny is then diversified by masculine air.

That which air disseminated leads to summer, when nurtured by water. In summer's three steps, feminine water's generation is ripened by masculine fire, whose yield is then serviced by feminine earth.

That which earth produced feeds into autumn, when moved by air. In autumn's three steps, masculine air's reorientation is stilled by feminine water, whose sediment is then transported by masculine fire.

That which fire circulated disappears into winter, when stabilized by earth. In winter's three steps, feminine earth's foundation is complemented by masculine air, whose framework is then enlivened by feminine water.

That which water quickened appears in spring, when emboldened by the return of fire. The dancers have now completed one circuit of the invisible braid through time. They, their progeny or their corpses then participate in another circuit.

Earth (see also Elements) ▽

Elemental earth is the stable support, the base that anchors the cycle of changes, which is entirely appropriate for the Earth as the still centre

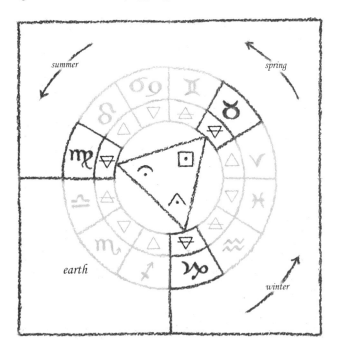

of the ever-spinning universe. It is a feminine element, the combination of dryness and cold. Earth introduced winter in Capricorn, was at the heart of spring in Taurus and bid farewell to summer in Virgo. Then, having set the scene, it played no further part in autumn.

Elements (see also Air, Earth, Fire, Qualities, Water)

Although the four traditional elements – fire, air, water and earth – are commonly attributed to Aristotle, they first appear in an enigmatic poem by Empedocles. Empedocles travelled far and it is probable that he got the idea from the shamans of central Asia.

The four elements are not like modern science's hundred or so elements, which are physical building blocks. Rather, they are the four ways of being in the world. Earth is the way of being stable and solid, water, the way of being fluid and heavy, air, the way of being fluid and light, while fire is the way of penetrating, redistributing and appearing to consume things.

The elements are expressions of combinations of four qualities: hot and cold, and wet and dry. Fire is dry and hot, air is hot and wet, water is wet and cold, earth is cold and dry. The order of the elements in an ideal world would be – descending from the heavens – fire, air, water and earth, with neighbouring spheres each sharing a quality. For example, fire and air share heat, air and water share moisture while water and earth share coldness. The elements also circulate through shared qualities. Elements that share qualities are 'concordant' while those that don't – for example, fire and water – are 'contrasting'.

In the sub-lunary world, the elements only ever appear in mixtures – although one element will always dominate – and compositions of mixed bodies change as they interact with their environments. Ideally, things that are predominantly fiery and airy are above, while predominantly watery and earthy things are below. If they find that they are not in their ideal homes, bodies will naturally rise or fall to get home.

This is an expression – at an elemental level – of the constant striving for perfection that characterizes the traditional cosmos.

Being closer to the celestial realms, fire and air are active, while, being closer to the chthonic realms, water and earth are receptive – fire and air 'act upon' water and earth, which are 'acted upon'. Fire and air are considered masculine or *yang*, while water and earth are feminine or *yin*.

A fifth element, ether, expresses the way of being in the heavens.

Fire (see also Elements) △

Elemental fire is the most active agent of change and drives transformations by appearing to consume things. It is a masculine element, the combination of dryness and heat. Fire introduced spring in Aries, was at the heart of summer in Leo and bid farewell to autumn in Sagittarius. Then, having set the scene, it played no further part in winter.

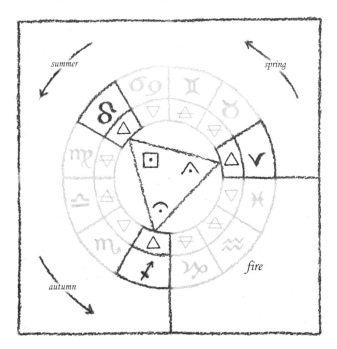

Fixed (see also Cardinal, Mutable, Seasons) ⊡

The fixed signs – Taurus (earth), Leo (fire), Scorpio (water) and Aquarius (air) – occur in the middle of a season. So, fixed earth (Taurus) is at the heart of spring, fixed fire (Leo), the heart of summer and fixed water (Scorpio), the heart of autumn, while fixed air (Aquarius) is the heart of winter.

Relative to the cardinal and mutable signs – when light levels change fast (either side of the equinoxes) and slowly (either side of the solstices) – the rate of change of light levels in the fixed signs is quite steady. The fixed signs of summer and winter, Leo and Aquarius, which follow the solstices with steadily accelerating change, are both masculine. The fixed signs of spring and autumn, Taurus and Scorpio, which follow the equinoxes with steadily decelerating change, are feminine. Like the cardinal signs, these four fixed signs also form a cross, dividing the year into four quarters.

The fixed signs each travel along the paths that were opened up by cardinal signs.

Form (see Hylomorphism)

Hylomorphism

Hylomorphism is the ancient Greek doctrine that all things consist of some matter (*hyle*) in some shape or form (*morph*). Some things may have very distinct shapes or forms with relatively little matter (like cumulus clouds) while others may seem to involve much matter and little form (like mud). But form and matter only exist in combination with each other – neither pure form nor pure matter exist. Pure matter is literally inconceivable since just trying to imagine it gives it some mental form. Likewise, pure form is unimaginable, as has been explored for millennia in apophatic theology or the 'negative way', which is the idea that God can only be approached through unknowing.

Form and matter are distinct but inseparable. The combinations of specific forms and matters are fluid so, for example, clouds change and so does mud. Seeds have forms and matters – those of the willow are light and fluffy and those of the oak are heavy and dense – and they turn into trees with different forms and matters. Trees, for their part, can also be turned into tables or chairs. In fact, one of the meanings of the word *hyle* was 'wood' since it was matter that could take many different forms.

Form and matter are the complementary constituents of everything – from the Underworld to the heavens, including us in the middle – and are the West's equivalents of the Eastern pair *yin* and *yang*. The zodiac signs alternate between elements that are masculine (*yang* and subtle, either fire or air) and feminine (*yin* and dense, either water and earth). They also alternate between elements that are 'friendly' or concordant (sharing a quality in common) and 'in strife' or contrasting (with no qualities in common). These alternations are expressions of Nature as a fabric woven of form and matter.

Jupiter (see also Planets) ♃

Jupiter's orbit is about twelve years. The ruler of Sagittarius and Pisces is often portrayed as a contented, portly late middle-aged gentleman who represents benevolence and generosity. Jupiter's expansive nature underlies the plenitude that enables exchange so that, for example, a tree can access nutrients from elsewhere in the forest. Jupiter's selfless sharing of slowly accumulated understanding also underlies the accessibility of Nature's information, so that snowflakes everywhere in the world, for example, know what shape to become.

Mars (see also Planets) ♂

Mars' orbit is about 22 months. The ruler of Aries and Scorpio is the god of war. Mars represents strife or the making of 'many from one' that, in combination with its opposite – making 'one from many', represented by Venus – is necessary for the preservation of life.

Matter (see Hylomorphism)

Mercury (see also Planets) ☿

Mercury's orbit is about 88 days. The ruler of Gemini and Virgo is often portrayed as a busy, athletic and androgynous youth. As the messenger of the gods, Mercury represents connection, communication and exchange. Mercury's exchanges tend to be quick and local, as opposed to Jupiter's slow and global ones, just as its rapid orbit contrasts with Jupiter's relatively slow one. Mercury governs the exchanges inherent in pollination and the aeration of soil, for example.

Moon (see also Planets) ☾

The Moon's orbit is about 28 days. The ruler of Cancer is often depicted as the Queen of the Night, consort of the Sun who is King of the Day. The Moon's orbit is closest to Earth and marks the boundary between the changing world of four elements and the unchanging heavens, the Realm of Becoming and the image of the Realm of Being. The Moon's unchanging rhythm of changes makes her the governor of change in the world.

Mutable (see also Cardinal, Fixed, Seasons) ⌢

The mutable signs – Gemini (air), Virgo (earth), Sagittarius (fire) and Pisces (water) – all occur at the end of a season. The mutable signs share out the qualities and goods accumulated through the fixed signs.

Like the cardinal and fixed signs, these four mutable signs also form a cross – with two opposed masculine signs, Gemini and Sagittarius, and two opposed feminine signs, Virgo and Pisces. The signs of this cross are ruled by the same two planets, with Mercury and Jupiter defining both members. Mercury rules spring and summer's Gemini and Virgo while Jupiter rules autumn and winter's Sagittarius and Pisces. Mercury is associated with short, quick changes while Jupiter is associated with long, slow changes. The mutable signs distribute what was gathered along the path opened by the cardinal sign and travelled by the fixed sign in each quadrant.

The mutable signs prepare the world for the changes of season that will occur with the solstices and equinoxes that follow them.

Planets (see also Jupiter, Mars, Mercury, Moon, Saturn, Sun and Venus)

The word 'planet' comes from the Greek for 'wanderer'. The planets are all those heavenly bodies that travel across the sky, moving against the backdrop of fixed stars. They are traditionally conceived as orbiting in concentric spheres around the Earth.

Modern astrology includes the planets that are not visible to the naked eye and were discovered more recently, using telescopes. Uranus (which was discovered in 1781 and was named after the classical lord of the sky) now rules Aquarius along with Saturn, and Neptune (classical lord of the sea, discovered in 1846) rules Pisces along with Jupiter, while Pluto (classical lord of darkness, discovered in 1930 and downgraded to dwarf in 2006) rules Scorpio, along with Mars. These outer planets are very slow-moving, with orbits of about

84, 165 and 248 years, respectively. They are generally associated with collective rather than individual, and societal rather than natural, issues, although of course these cannot be hard distinctions.

Qualities (see also Elements)

The four fundamental qualities are hot and cold, and wet and dry. The combination of cold and dry manifests as the stable, solid way of being or elemental earth. The combination of cold and wet is the dense fluid, or watery, way of being. Hot and wet are the subtle fluid, or airy, way of being while hot and dry are the consuming, or fiery, way of being.

Realms of Being and Becoming (see also Three Worlds)

The Realm of Being corresponds to the heavens, from the sphere of the Moon upwards. It contains the orbits of the planets which provide a basis for measuring time, the moving image of an unchanging eternity. The Realm of Becoming corresponds to the Earth, centre of the traditional universe, and the location of constant change, of coming into being, of passing away and of the unceasing metamorphoses of all things made from the four elements. The two realms correspond to the outside and inside of Plato's Cave (*Republic*, VII).

Retrograde

A planet is described as retrograde when it appears to travel from west to east – as opposed to its usual east-to-west movement – against the backdrop of fixed stars. Inner planets are retrograde less often than outer planets. Mercury is retrograde for about three weeks, three times a year; Venus about six weeks, five times every eight years; and Mars about two months, every other year. Jupiter is retrograde about four months every nine months, and Saturn about four-and-a-half months every year.

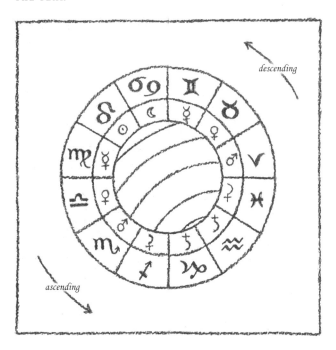

Ruler (see also Planets, Signs)

In the traditional zodiac, each sign is ruled by one of the seven visible planets. The 'luminaries' each rule one sign, and the Sun rules Leo while the Moon rules Cancer. The other five planets each rule two signs. Mercury rules Gemini and Virgo, Venus rules Taurus and Libra, Mars rules Aries and Scorpio, Jupiter rules Pisces and Sagittarius, while Saturn rules Aquarius and Capricorn. The ruling planets are in the same order as their nested orbits in the Ptolemaic universe. On one side of the zodiac's fixed cross – from Aquarius to Cancer – the signs descend the planetary ladder. On the other side of the cross – from Leo to Capricorn – the signs reascend the planetary ladder.

Saturn (see also Planets) ♄

Saturn's orbit is about 29 years. The ruler of Capricorn and Aquarius is depicted as an old man and sometimes – as the god of time – he is shown eating his children. The planet's distance from the Sun and the Earth gives Saturn a cold and slow disposition, appropriate for the winter months but also alluding to the unhurried and dispassionate nature of wisdom.

Seasons (see also Cardinal, Fixed, Mutable, Signs, Zodiac)

The four seasons result from two different ways of dividing the zodiac in half – into light and dark halves as well as ascending and descending halves. The light half is between the spring and autumn equinoxes, or from Aries to Virgo. The dark half is between the autumn and spring equinoxes, or from Libra to Pisces. The ascending half (of increasing light or decreasing dark) is between the winter and summer solstices, or from Capricorn to Gemini, while the descending half (of decreasing light or increasing dark) is between the summer and winter solstice, or from Cancer to Sagittarius. Combining the light-and-dark halves with the ascending-and-descending halves makes four qualitatively different seasons.

Spring (between the spring equinox and summer solstice) consists of Aries, Taurus and Gemini, when light predominates and the days are growing. Summer (between the summer solstice and autumn equinox) consists of Cancer, Leo and Virgo, when light predominates but the days are shrinking. Autumn (between the autumn equinox and winter solstice) consists of Libra, Scorpio and Sagittarius, when darkness predominates and the days are shrinking. Winter (between the winter solstice and spring equinox) consists of Capricorn, Aquarius and Pisces, when darkness predominates but the days are growing.

The seasons are not equally long. Callippus, a contemporary of Aristotle, determined their respective lengths at 94, 92, 89 and 90 days, to the nearest whole day.

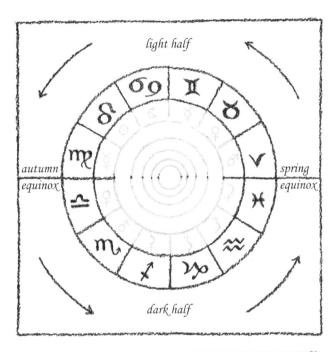

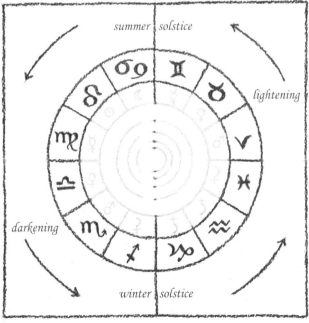

Signs (see also Cardinal, Elements, Fixed, Mutable, Seasons, Zodiac)

The zodiac signs, also known as Sun signs, are the origin of our calendar months. They are the parts of the sky where the Sun resides during particular months of its annual circuit. Of course, the constellations associated with the signs are in the sky during the day so cannot be seen. Instead, at night, we see the constellations associated with the zodiac's opposite signs, like Libra and its neighbours during Aries, for example.

The signs are either cardinal, fixed or mutable, marking each season's beginning, middle and end. Spread across the year, each sign is also one of three stages in the expression of the four elements, or modes of being in the world.

Spring (see also Seasons)

Spring comes into being with fire in Aries, has earth at its heart in Taurus, and passes away with air in Gemini. Its rulers – Mars, Venus and Mercury, respectively – are moving progressively closer to Earth. Spring is when the light dominates and continues to increase.

Summer (see also Seasons)

Summer comes into being with water in Cancer, has fire at its heart in Leo, and passes away with earth in Virgo. Its rulers – the Moon, Sun and Mercury, respectively – are the two luminaries and the non-luminary planet closest to Earth. (The Sun's orbit is actually in the centre of the seven planets' orbits in the geocentric system and, as the centre, it transcends the others. After all, no one law rules Nature and some fish fly while some birds swim.) Summer is when the light dominates but darkness starts to increase.

Sun (see also Planets) ⊙

By definition, in the geocentric universe, the Sun's orbit is one year. In terms of modern cosmology, the Earth orbits the Sun in one year, yet the Sun is not still. It orbits the centre of the Milky Way about once every 230 million years, slowly deconstructing the constellations as seen from Earth. But, back in the geocentric universe, the ruler of Leo orbits at the very centre of the nested heavenly spheres, midway between Earth and the fixed stars. Its centrality, along with the fact that it is the only luminous planet, makes it transcend the others in status. (The other luminary, the Moon, merely reflects its light.) The Sun's influence on Earth is greater than any other planet and it empowers all the other planets, especially its immediate neighbours, Mars and Venus.

Teleology

Teleology is the idea of a purposeful movement towards some end or goal. For Aristotle, the driving force of events below the sphere of the Moon (in the Realm of Becoming) was the pursuit of perfection. For him, this perfection was one consequence of his observation that 'the whole is different from the sum of its parts'. In etymology, *per-fect* means 'through, or by means of, making' from the Proto-Indian-European root meaning 'forward', chief or first.

Modern science has difficulties with teleology, but it can also recognize that 'the whole can be different from the sum of its parts' in the case of complex and adaptable 'self-organizing' systems with 'emergent properties'. In culture, emergent properties include traffic jams and stock-market crashes. In Nature, emergent properties include swarms of bees and flocks of birds, as well as 'problem solving' behaviours, like fungi finding the shortest route to food and ants finding the greatest distance to dispose of their dead. Yet modern science also has some difficulties with the idea of self-organizing systems and emergent properties.

Religious worldviews avoid modern science's quandaries by seeing the world as a visible manifestation of God, a 'theophany'. In the Christian tradition, the Book of Nature is the second scripture. In the Islamic tradition, God was a hidden treasure who wished to be known (and can be at least partly known through Nature). Everyday perfections – like the fungi that find the shortest route to their food and the ants that find the greatest distance to dispose of their dead – are tiny glimpses of the divine. On the other hand, perfections at the end of cosmic cycles – the Hindu days of Brahma, for example – are fuller revelations. The former perfections are relatively knowable, cataphatic and affirming, while the latter perfections are unknowable, or apophatic and negating. Both contain mysteries.

Three Worlds (see also Dance, Realms of Being and Becoming)

The traditional idea of three worlds softens the hard binary of two realms, the Realms of Being and Becoming.

The chthonic Underworld, which is traditionally dark, is the lowest of the three traditional worlds. The highest world is the celestial heavens, which are traditionally light and represented by the planets and stars. The world we occupy is between these two, an intermediate, liminal realm that is influenced by both the light and the dark, the higher and lower worlds. In the zodiac, our world is fed in strict order, alternating input from above (fire and air signs) and below (water and earth signs).

In modern ecology, our intermediate realm corresponds to the 'biosphere', a thin, porous zone which engages with both the geological regions below and the atmospheric regions above.

Venus (see also Planets) ♀

Venus' orbit is about 225 days. The ruler of Taurus and Libra is the goddess of love. Venus represents love or the making of 'one from many' that, in combination with its opposite – making 'many from one', represented by Mars – is necessary for the preservation of life.

Water (see also Elements) ▽

Elemental water is the dense fluid that is ever-receptive because it goes where it is willed and carries whatever it encounters. It is a feminine element, the combination of moisture and cold. Water introduced summer in Cancer, was at the heart of autumn in Scorpio, and bid farewell to winter in Pisces. Then, having set the scene, it played no further part in spring.

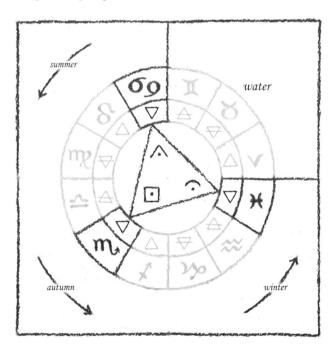

Winter (see also Seasons)

Winter comes into being with earth in Libra, has air at its heart in Aquarius, and passes away with water in Pisces. Its rulers – Saturn (in feminine mode), Saturn (in masculine mode) and Jupiter – are the furthest from Earth and are the slowest-moving. Winter is when the dark dominates but light starts to increase.

Zodiac (see also Hylomorphism, Seasons, Signs)

The zodiac connects the large and small orders of Nature. It provides a framework for time, the container of events and processes. It maps finely tuned dynamic balances between light and dark, heat and cold, dryness and wetness, mobility and immobility, gravity and levity, action and reception. The order that emerges from those interconnections reveals itself as four seasons and twelve signs. Traditionally, a profound beauty was seen to emerge from the zodiac's order, fitness-for-purpose and mandala-like unity.

As time unfolds, cosmic lightness and darkness increase and decrease in steady rhythms. Below the Moon, on Earth, the container of events – the fabric of time – takes a woven structure. Its warp threads are spun from alternating heat and cold, the sub-lunary effects of cosmic light and dark, while its weft threads are spun from alternating dryness and wetness. As a liminal zone, our world – the thin biosphere – hovers between the heavens and the Underworld, and is fed repeatedly in strict order, from above (channelled through hot-and-dry fire, or hot-and-wet air) and from below (through cold-and-wet water, or cold-and-dry earth).

The zodiac's weaving together of alternating qualities and influences mirrors hylomorphism and is mirrored in Nature's reciprocity, from massive trees and their hidden mycorrhizal partners to the modest entanglements we call lichen. The dynamics within the Realm of Becoming are achieved by weaving together life's two great pathways, the grazing food chain (which builds up) and the detrital food chain (which breaks down).

Metaphysically, the zodiac suggests a crystallized structure for terrestrial time, the 'moving image of eternity'. The twelve signs are like the twelve gates of the Babylonian-influenced Heavenly Jerusalem (Revelation 21). The biblical city is a cube with twelve foundations and with three gates facing each of the four directions. The three gates on each side – one for each of the 'tribes' in the city's quarters – correspond to the three stages – cardinal, fixed and mutable – through which each season unfolds. Moving through the twelve months of the year is like a rehearsal for ritually progressing around the heavenly city, rosary in hand, each gate or bead corresponding to a sign.

The zodiac is a choreographic structure containing the ever-improvised dance of time, from sign to sign, season to season, and aeon to aeon, its rhythm of opposites circulating through countless permutations. The natural and worldly events that we encounter – and which we only glimpse partially, fragmented through time, across days, months and decades – can all be reconciled within its structure.

REFERENCES

PROLOGUE: *Ecology and the Zodiac*

1 Of course, people also shape places. See, for example, D. Bhattacharyya, *Empire and Ecology in the Bengal Delta* (Cambridge, 2018). Most cities developed around places where nature offered resources and enabled communication. However, those changes were intentional and are a part of another story. The Epilogue will touch upon some unintended ways in which people are now shaping places.

2 R. Foster and L. Kreitzman, *Circadian Rhythms* (Oxford, 2017), pp. 119–21.

3 Preliterate ancient (and literate premodern) observers of nature enjoyed two advantages over those who observe nature today. Unlike us, they had cultural stability and strong oral traditions which together allowed the accumulation and refining of natural observations over multiple generations. See references in the First Interlude, note 2, and the Epilogue, note 12.

4 And that's true if you live in the southern hemisphere. But in the northern hemisphere, the Sun is approx. 152 million kilometres (94 million mi.) away during the summer and only approx. 147 million kilometres (91 million mi.) away during the winter. The experience of a person in the northern hemisphere therefore runs counter to what modern science might seem to suggest, although, in reality, the 5-million-kilometre (3-million-mi.) difference is negligible compared to other factors.

5 Nature was repackaged as a clockwork mechanism, devoid of spirit. Ways of marginalizing previous views of nature included dismissing them as 'old wives' tales' and prioritizing texts over oral traditions. These historic strategies help account for the gender imbalance in the authorities cited throughout this book.

6 This book eschews the BCE (Before Common Era) and CE (Common Era) date convention since that is part of the modern repackaging of a secularized nature. The BC (Before Christ) and AD (Anno Domini)

convention is one possible way of acknowledging a spiritual dimension to time. Other date conventions relevant to the Western zodiac's development include the Islamic BH (Before the Hijra) and AH (Anno Hegirae), and the AM (Anno Mundi) of the Hebrew calendar, which itself has Babylonian roots.

7 There are other start-dates. From the seventeenth century, English *Gardeners' Kalendars* started in November, and the school year still starts after the harvest has been gathered.

8 See, for example, A. Cunningham, 'How the *Principia* Got Its Name', *History of Science*, XXIX/4 (1991), pp. 377–92, and A. Cunningham, 'The Identity of Natural Philosophy', *Early Science and Medicine*, V/3 (2000), pp. 259–78.

9 For a seventeenth-century example, see B. S. Orlove et al., 'Forecasting Andean Rainfall and Crop Yield from the Influence of El Niño on Pleiades Visibility', *Nature*, CDIII/6765 (2000), pp. 68–71.

10 Heaven's 'unvarying revolutions' have also been translated as 'revolutions of intelligence', compared with the 'troubled revolutions of our understanding'.

ONE: March–April

1 As it stands, the book tells one four-part story: the story of spring, summer, autumn and winter. But it is also a collection of four, three-part stories. They are the story of fire (with its beginning, middle and end in Chapters 1, 5 and 9); the story of earth (Chapters 10, 2 and 6); the story of air (Chapters 7, 11 and 3); and the story of water (Chapters 4, 8 and 12). There are also five couplets – about Mars (Chapters 1 and 8), Venus (Chapters 2 and 7), Mercury (Chapters 3 and 6), Jupiter (Chapters 9 and 12) and Saturn (Chapters 10 and 11) – as well as one Solar story (Chapter 5) and one Lunar story (Chapter 4).

2 In the spirit of two beginnings for the year, thorns can also blossom at Christmas. In fact, after the British adopted the Gregorian calendar in 1752, the blossoming of cuttings from Glastonbury's Holy Thorn – an off-shoot of Joseph of Arimathea's staff – was used to test Christmas's true date. The tree observed the 'Old-Stile' year, blossoming on 5 January. *The Gentleman's Magazine*, XXIII/1 (1753), p. 49.

3 But Thoreau, for example, did consult centuries-old European reports of Indigenous peoples' observations of nature. B. P. Dean, 'Annotating the "Jesuit Relations" Parts I and II', *Thoreau Society Bulletin*, CCXLII (2003), pp. 1–3 and CCXLIII (2003), pp. 6–9. And, to date, while the modern West has been willing to appropriate other cultures' knowledge, it has been reluctant to acknowledge those cultures' contributions to science. See, for example, A. E. Slaton

and T. Saraiva, 'Editorial', *History and Technology*, xxxix/2 (2023), pp. 127–36.

4 This month's ruler, for example, is reflected in iron, the metal traditionally associated with weaponry.

5 C. W. Whippo and R. Hangarter, 'Phototropism; Bending towards Enlightenment', *The Plant Cell*, xviii/5 (2006), pp. 1,110–19.

two: April–May

1 The mulberry told gardeners when the dangers had receded because the 'Wise Tree' only unfurled its leaves after the last frost had come and gone.

2 I. Adler, *Solving the Riddle of Phyllotaxis* (Singapore, 2012).

3 Although Venus' orbit is much closer to being a perfect circle than Earth's orbit.

4 It is perhaps significant that the modern fertilizers and pesticides have their origins in a chemical industry that developed to serve the military.

5 A. C. Gaskett et al., 'Orchid Sexual Deceit Provokes Ejaculation', *The American Naturalist*, clxxi/6 (2008), e206–12.

6 E. A. Herre et al., 'Evolutionary Ecology of Figs and Their Associates', *Annual Review of Ecology, Evolution and Systematics*, xxxix/1 (2008), pp. 439–58.

three: May–June

1 See R. L. Vadas, 'The Anatomy of an Ecological Controversy', *Oikos*, lxix/1 (1994), pp. 158–66; T. Munz, 'The Bee Battles', *Journal of the History of Biology*, xxxviii/3 (2005), pp. 535–70; and S. Crist, 'Can an Insect Speak?', *Social Studies of Science*, xxxiv/1 (2004), pp. 7–43.

2 D.J.G. Pearce et al., 'Role of Projection in the Control of Bird Flocks', *Proceedings of the National Academy of Sciences of the United States of America*, cxi/29 (2014), pp. 10,422–6.

3 About that other social insect, the bee, Shakespeare wrote of 'singing masons building roofs of gold', *Henry v* (i, ii). Shakespeare's 'singing' suggests that the 'masons' are not slavishly following the instructions of an unseen architect but are instead enchanted by – or literally 'in 'in the song of ' – the hive, playing their part in concert with their fellow bees.

4 E. Bonabeau et al., 'A Model for the Emergence of Pillars, Walls and Royal Chambers in Termite Nests', *Philosophical Transactions: Biological Sciences*, ccliii/1375 (1998), pp. 1,561–76.

5 S. J. Martin et al., 'A Vast 4,000-year-old Spatial Pattern of Termite Mounds', *Current Biology*, xxviii/22 (2018), pp. 1,292–3.

6 A. Walton et al., 'Variation in Individual Worker Honey Bee Behaviour Shows Hallmarks of Personality', *Behavioural Ecology and Sociobiology*, LXX/7 (2016), pp. 999–1,010.

7 The flock can grow as the dance proceeds, which suggests that the birds may be advertising suitable roosting sites for their neighbours to share. 'Making one from many' would traditionally be seen as an act of love. The birds protect themselves from predators by flying closer together on the flock's vulnerable margins.

8 Humility, because the Christian dragon was a symbol of the tyrannical ego. In other cultures, the dragon has much more positive roles, many of them related to natural forces.

9 Q. Li et al., 'A Day Trip in the Forest Park Increases Human Natural Killer Activity', *Journal of Biological Regulators and Homeostatic Agents*, XXIV/2 (2010), pp. 157–65, and E. J. Flies et al., 'Biodiverse Green Spaces: A Prescription for Global Health', *Frontiers in Ecology and the Environment*, XV/9 (2017), pp. 510–16.

10 Summer Allen, 'The Science of Awe', John Templeton Foundation and Greater Good Science Center, Berkeley, www.ggsc.berkeley.edu, September 2018.

FIRST INTERLUDE

1 The word 'interlude' means 'between play'. This interlude lies between the games that nature plays when light increases through a period dominated by light (spring) and those played when light still dominates but light is receding (summer). A second interlude will lie between summer's play and the games nature plays when light continues to decrease through a period dominated by darkness (autumn). A third will lie between autumn's play and the games played when darkness still dominates but darkness is receding (winter).

2 B. C. Ray, 'Stonehenge, a New Theory', *History of Religions*, XXVI/3 (1987), pp. 225–78.

FOUR: June–July

1 Of course, this rhythm of life is repeated in every sign, not just in the sign ruled by the Moon. But flying fish, swimming birds and ivy's skototropism and phototropism, for example, all show that the natural world is complex. The traditional sciences accommodate nature's complexities by recognizing that, though there are twelve signs and seven rulers etc., no natural phenomenon – whether human, animal, vegetable or mineral – can be fully accounted for by any one of them. A modern echo of this age-old

principle is the concept of intersectionality, which suggests that no individual can be fully defined by any one social category, such as race or gender.

2 S. Hernandez-Leon et al., 'Carbon Sequestration and Zooplankton Lunar Cycles', *Limnology and Oceanography*, LV/6 (2010), pp. 2,503–12, and N. Kronfeld-Schor et al., 'Chronobiology by Moonlight', *Proceedings: Biological Sciences*, CCLXXX/1765 (2013), pp. 1–11.

3 K. A. Vogt, 'Indigenous Knowledge Informing Management of Tropical Forests', *Ambio*, XXXI/6 (2002), pp. 485–90.

4 Mid-twentieth-century science may have dismissed lunar correlations, but those who worked with nature still saw them. For example, when working as a fire look-out in America's northwest in the 1950s, Jack Kerouac's Ray Smith noted that 'all the insects ceased in honor of the moon' (*The Dharma Bums*, 33).

5 I. Billick et al., 'The Relationship between Ant-Tending and Maternal Care in the Treehopper', *Behavioural Ecology and Sociobiology*, LI/1 (2001), pp. 41–6.

6 T. D. Seeley et al., 'Group Decision Making in Honey Bee Swarms', *American Scientist*, XCIV/3 (2006), pp. 220–29.

7 S. W. Mintz, *Sweetness and Power* (New York, 1985), and M. Sahlins et al., 'The Sadness of Sweetness', *Current Anthropology*, XXXVII/3 (1996), pp. 395–428.

8 L. Sims, 'Entering, and Returning from, the Underworld', *Journal of the Royal Anthropological Institute*, XV/2 (2009), pp. 386–408. But see also C. Chippindale, 'Stoned Henge: Events and Issues at the Summer Solstice, 1985', *World Archaeology*, XVIII/1 (1986), pp. 38–58.

FIVE: July–August

1 P. E. Stander, 'Cooperative Hunting in Lions', *Behavioral Ecology and Sociobiology*, XXIX/6 (1992), pp. 445–54, and C. Packer, A. Pusey and L. Eberly, 'Egalitarianism in Female African Lions', *Science*, NS, CCXCIII/5530 (2001), pp. 690–93.

2 Chess originated in India, where it was a game of the gods, and in Persia it helped educate kings and the nobility. Some very early chess pieces were animal-headed and the rook/rukh was a mythical animal. Parallels with the natural world are therefore not surprising.

3 M. Bhargava, 'Of Orcas and Otters', *Ecology Law Quarterly*, XXXII/4 (2005), pp. 939–88.

4 Marine micro-organisms are extraordinarily varied compared, for example, with orca. This pyramidal distribution of species reflects earthly multiplicity and heavenly unity and is the metaphysical basis for the idea of monarchies, whether human or animal.

5 J. L. Clasen and J. B. Shurin, 'Kelp Forest Size Alters Microbial Community and Function', *Ecology*, XCVI/3 (2015), pp. 862–72.

6 G. V. Hildebrand et al., 'Role of Brown Bears in the Flow of Marine Nitrogen into a Terrestrial Ecosystem', *Oecologia*, CXXI/4 (1999), pp. 546–50.

7 J. A. Estes et al., 'Trophic Downgrading of Planet Earth', *Science*, CCCXXXIII/6040 (2011), pp. 301–6.

8 Many of our ecological problems stem from vantage points that privilege products over processes, for example, great whales (as resources) over interactions within multispecies communities.

9 Gilbert White, *The Natural History of Selborne*, ed. Anne Secord (Oxford, 2013), pp. 38–9 and 153.

10 Lubbock's leisure time was very fruitful. In addition to instigating holidays, saving heritage and studying ants, he was also well read – he compiled the first, and surprisingly diverse, list of '100 best books' – and, relevant to the zodiac, he designed and constructed a star-chart in 1870. Unlike the illustrations in this book, which depict the constellations as if seen from outside the sphere of fixed stars, his chart depicts them from within the sphere, as we see them, appropriate for a work published 'under the superintendence of the Society for the Diffusion of Useful Knowledge'. There is always more than one way of looking at anything, even a distant constellation.

SIX: August–September

1 This is a subterranean version of the cross-species maternal care between ants and aphids we saw in Cancer.

2 P. B. Thomas et al., 'The Interaction of Temperature, Water Availability and Fire Cue', *Oecologia*, CLXII/2 (2010), pp. 293–302; G. S. Liyanage et al., 'Seedling Performance Covaries with Dormancy Thresholds', *Ecology*, XCVII/11 (2016), pp. 3,009–18; and R. V. Gallagher et al., 'High Fire Frequency and the Impact of the 2019–20 Megafires', *Diversity and Distributions*, XXVII/7 (2021), pp. 1,166–79.

3 J. Yoshimura, 'The Evolutionary Origins of Periodical Cicadas during Ice Ages', *American Naturalist*, CXLIX/1 (1997), pp. 112–24.

4 P. White, 'Darwin's Emotions', *Isis*, C/4 (2009), pp. 811–26.

5 Gilbert White, *The Natural History of Selborne*, ed. Anne Secord (Oxford, 2013), p. 173.

6 E. S. Reed, 'Darwin's Earthworms', *Behaviorism*, X/2 (1982), pp. 165–85.

SECOND INTERLUDE

1 See 'Seasons' in the Glossary.

SEVEN: September–October

1 In the context moving between two realms, and the month that introduces the dark half of the year – the annual equivalent of the daily transition between the time of the dog and the time of the wolf – it may be significant that the village's name is a contraction of 'Wolf-pit', a pit for trapping wolves.

2 Of course, copper and children occupy different links in the Great Chain of Being, so their relationship with air differs. Air that potentially causes both the loss and gaining of green is consistent with the cosmic Law of Inversion.

3 T. A. Blackledge, 'Spider Silk: A Brief Review and Prospectus', *Journal of Arachnology*, XL/1 (2012), pp. 1–12.

4 See, for example, Gordon Deegan, 'Fairy Bush Survives the Motorway Planners', *Irish Times*, www.irishtimes.com, 29 May 1999, and Associated Press Reykjavik, 'Elf Lobby Blocks Iceland Road Project', *The Guardian*, www.theguardian.com, 22 December 2013.

5 J. M. Gomez, 'Spatial Patterns in Long Distance Dispersal', *Ecography*, XXVI/5 (2003), pp. 573–84.

EIGHT: October–November

1 C. Zaleski, *Otherworld Journeys: Accounts of Near-Death Experience in Medieval and Modern Times* (Oxford, 1987).

2 *Trophic Ecology: Bottom-Up and Top-Down Interactions*, ed. T. C. Hanley and K. J. LaPierre (Cambridge, 2015).

3 C. E. Yorke et al., 'Sea Urchins Mediate the Availability of Kelp Detritus', *Proceedings: Biological Sciences*, CCLXXXVI/1906 (2019), pp. 1–8.

4 M. E. Benbow et al., 'Necrobiome Framework for Bridging Decomposition Ecology', *Ecological Monographs*, LXXXIX/1 (2019), pp. 1–29.

5 R.L.M. Lee, 'Modernity, Mortality and Re-Enchantment: The Death Taboo Revisited', *Sociology*, XLII/4 (2008), pp. 745–59.

6 While spring and autumn's fixed signs are both feminine, the fixed signs of summer and winter – fire and air, respectively – are both masculine.

7 Metempsychosis in vegetables also prevented devout Manichees from killing plants. See A. Henrichs, 'Thou Shalt Not Kill a Tree', *Bulletin of the American Society of Papyrologists*, XVI/1–2 (1979), pp. 83–108.

8 On the other hand, Sampson's riddle – 'out of the strong came forth sweetness' – suggested that bees emerged from lions, which, being (seemingly) lazy, could not be the source of the bees' devotion to toil. See Judges 14:14.

9 R. E. Antwis et al., eds, *Microbiomes of Soils, Plants and Animals* (Cambridge, 2020).

10 J. F. Cryan et al., 'Mind-Altering Microorganisms: The Impact of the Gut Microbiota on Brain and Behaviour', *Nature Reviews Neuroscience*, XIII/10 (2012), pp. 701–12.

11 S. F. Gilbert et al., 'A Symbiotic View of Life: We Have Never Been Individuals', *Quarterly Review of Biology*, LXXXVII/4 (2012), pp. 325–41.

NINE: November–December

1 Jupiter will also rule the next mutable sign, Pisces, the end of winter, again in the dark half of the year.

2 S. E. Smith and D. J. Read, *Mycorrhizal Symbiosis* (Cambridge, MA, 2008).

3 D. Yih, 'Food, Poison and Espionage', *Arnoldia*, LXXV/2 (2017), pp. 2–11. In modern ecology it has become increasingly difficult to avoid the teleological assumptions of the traditional sciences.

4 D. W. Wolfe, *Tales from the Underground* (New York, 2002).

5 The fire that touched gunpowder originally came from the pistol's flint. Flint will be considered in the next chapter, under an earth sign. In the terms of modern science, gunpowder rapidly generates large volumes of nitrogen and carbon dioxide ($3C + S + 2KNO_3 \rightarrow K_2S + N_2 + 3CO_2$). Modern gunpowder is nitrocellulose which, as its name suggests, is derived from plant matter. Most modern explosives are derived from oil, which contains the fossilized solar energy harvested by whole forests.

THIRD INTERLUDE

1 Dáithí Ó hÓgáin, *The Lore of Ireland: An Encyclopaedia of Myth, Legend and Romance* (Woodbridge, 2006).

TEN: December–January

1 The modern world recognizes slower planets, but Saturn is the slowest that is visible to the naked eye.

2 Persephone had to remain in the Underworld for half a year because she broke her fast there, picking a pomegranate and eating seven seeds (or maybe garnets; Ovid, *Metamorphoses*, v). For well over a millennium, the West African goldfields have been considered 'subterranean granaries' that saw people through times of famine. The gold was

controlled by 'spirit snakes' who demanded sacrifices, while gold-bearing rock was actively shared across the community and with the as yet unborn. Industrial mining is now killing off this ancient way of life. See R. D'Avignon, *A Ritual Geology* (Durham, NC, and London, 2020), pp. 58–85.

3 F. Barry, *Painting in Stone* (New Haven, CT, 2020), pp. 49–63.

4 R. G. Bromley and A. A. Ekdale, 'Trace Fossil Preservation in European Chalk', *Journal of Paleontology*, LVIII/2 (1984), pp. 298–311.

5 In terms of modern chemistry: roasting lime, $CaCO_3 \rightarrow CaO + CO_2$; slaking lime, $CaO + H_2O \rightarrow Ca(OH)_2$; recarbonation, $Ca(OH)_2 + CO_2 \rightarrow CaCO_3 + H_2O$.

6 C. F. Demoulin et al., 'Cyanobacteria Evolution', *Free Radical Biology and Medicine*, CXL (2019), pp. 206–23, and W. Li et al., 'Biologically Recycled Iron Is a Major Component in Banded Iron Formations', *Proceedings of the National Academy of Sciences*, CXII/27 (2015), pp. 8,193–8.

7 Vinegar's penetrating heat is evident in its sharp taste while urine's is evident in burning nappy rash.

8 A simplified version of the synthesis of lead white/lead carbonate proceeds via lead acetate: $2Pb + 4CH_3COOH + O_2 \rightarrow 2Pb(CH_3COO)_2 + 2H_2O$ followed by $Pb(CH_3COO)_2 + CO_2 + 2H_2O \rightarrow PbCO_3 + 2CH_3COOH$.

9 Of course, exchanges between Realms occur at any time and at all times, and Dante chose to place his epic journey in Holy Week across Easter, connecting it to Christ's death and resurrection.

10 The competing 'History of Religions' and 'Calculation' theories of Christmas's origins have been debated since at least the sixteenth century.

ELEVEN: January–February

1 See the work of diverse philosophers of science from, for example, Alfred North Whitehead, *Process and Reality* (Cambridge, 1929) to Deboleena Roy, *Molecular Feminisms* (Seattle, WA, 2018). See also *Neo-Aristotelian Perspectives on Contemporary Science*, ed. W.M.R. Simpson et al. (New York and London, 2018).

2 Physicists have proposed quarks and gluons, strings, quantum loop gravity and yet other ways of looking at what makes up protons and neutrons etc. But see W. Smith, *The Quantum Enigma* (New York, 2005).

3 K. Spalding et al., 'Retrospective Birth Dating of Cells in Humans', *Cell*, CXXII/1 (2005), pp. 133–43.

4 L. Gimeno et al., 'Atmospheric Rivers: A Mini-Review', *Frontiers in Earth Science, Atmospheric Science*, II (2014).

5 Of course, above the sphere of the Moon, heavenly forces came through a sea of ether, not air.

6 See, for example, *After Science and Religion*, ed. P. Harrison and J. Millbank (Cambridge, 2022).

7 The idea of 'wintering into wisdom' is in accord with the wider analogy between annual and daily cycles – spring is to morning as summer is to noon, autumn to evening and winter to night. In Italy it is said that 'night is the time of counsel' or 'night is the sea of thought', and in English it is said that you can solve a problem if you 'sleep on it'. W. B. Yeats noted that 'Though leaves are many, the root is one' and saw that, later, 'Now I may wither into truth' (*The Coming of Wisdom with Time*).

8 In fact, double-helix DNA comes in three different forms, A-, B- and left-handed Z-DNA. But DNA also comes as single and triple helices and quadruplex forms, as well as in junctions, loops, folds and more (see, for example, S. Neidle, 'Beyond the Double Helix', *Journal of Biological Chemistry*, CCXCVI/9 (2021), art. 100,553). There is also 'junk' or 'nonfunctional' DNA, which has been the subject of sometimes heated debate for over seventy years. Part of the problem is that different scientists have different ideas about what constitutes 'function', which, for them, is an uncomfortably teleological concept. The role of 'conserved noncoding elements' in DNA is uncertain, but they hold evidence of our connections with other species. See, for example, Nicole A. Leypold et al., 'Evolutionary Conservation in Noncoding Genomic Regions', *Trends in Genetics*, XXXVII/10 (2021), pp. 903–18.

9 Earth and air also met across the end of summer and beginning of autumn, where they were followed by fixed water. Mythologically, that meeting – between mutable earth and cardinal air – resonated with the release of Aeolus' winds. This month's meeting – between cardinal earth and fixed air – resonates with the recharging of Aeolus' winds. The other opposed elements, water and fire, also meet across the end of winter and beginning of spring, where they will be followed by fixed earth. Transitions between the twelve signs play out a complex rhythm of 3 × 4 elements, expressing all possibilities.

TWELVE: February–March

1 D. J. Beerling and P. J. Franks, 'The Hidden Cost of Transpiration', *Nature*, CDLXIV/7288 (2010), pp. 495–6.

2 The quality of homeopathic remedies – achieved by repeatedly diluting substances carried in water – is more 'formal' than hard water's grossly 'material' deposits. However, both involve everyday physical water and therefore can only approximately allude to Aquarius' mutable elemental

waters. The same caveat should also be applied to the watery processes that were used to illustrate the zodiac's cardinal and fixed waters, along with all the fiery, earthy and airy processes described in earlier chapters.

3 H. R. Brown, 'The Theory of the Rise of Sap in Trees', *Physics in Perspective*, xv/3 (2013), pp. 320–58.

4 Watt harnessed the power of water as it changed from a vapour to a liquid. The fracturing of trees and rocks was an expression of the power of water as it changed from a liquid to a solid. These abrupt changes of phase are collective behaviours that involve individual molecules of water exchanging information with their immediate neighbours. Freeze–thaw and evaporating–condensing could be seen as mineral versions of animal behaviours like starling murmuration.

5 Chairs and works of art are mainly made in the Realm of Becoming (which is within time). Natural things are made by more direct interactions with the Realm of Being (which is beyond time).

6 There are many different possible definitions of the soul and it is not immortal in all traditions. In the Hebrew and early Christian traditions the soul 'cleaveth unto the dust' and 'melteth away' (Psalm 119:25, 28) and the only immortal is God, 'Lord of the living and the dead' (Romans 14:9).

7 S. Bucklow, 'Silver, the Lunar Metal', in *Silver*, ed. H. Hills (Oxford, 2023), pp. 91–107.

FOURTH INTERLUDE

1 Symbolically, Christ's life on Earth marked cycles in time, binding religious rituals to nature's rhythms.

2 This interlude lies between the games played last year and those that will be played next year, which – in terms of the interplay between darkness and light – will be another game of four quarters.

EPILOGUE: *Next Year*

1 The water-to-fire transition marks the end of one eight-hundred-year cycle and the beginning of the next because the last month of the year is a water sign, Pisces, and the first month of the next is a fire sign, Aries.

2 The personification of winds has recently returned with the naming of those Atlantic storms whose death-throes now periodically wreak havoc on northwest Europe.

3 R. H. Thurstan, S. Brockington and C. M. Roberts, 'The Effects of 118 Years of Industrial Fishing', *Nature Communications*, I/15 (2010), pp. 1–6.

4 Gilbert White, *The Natural History of Selborne*, ed. Anne Secord (Oxford, 2013), p. 49.

5 Y. Cui et al., 'Massive and Rapid Predominantly Volcanic CO_2 Emission during the End-Permian Mass Extinction', *Proceedings of the National Academy of Science*, CXVIII/37 (2021), e201470118.

6 J. L. Penn et al., 'Temperature-Dependent Hypoxia Explains Biogeography and Severity of End-Permian Marine Mass Extinction', *Science*, CCCLXII/6419 (2018).

7 J-F. Bastin et al., 'Understanding Climate Change from a Global Analysis of City Analogues', *PLOSOne* (2019), and A. and R. Fitter, 'Rapid Changes in Flowering Time in British Plants', *Science*, CCXCVI/5573 (2002), pp. 1,689–91.

8 The Buddhist tradition shares those timeframes. For example, the Buddha Shakyamuni was born in the sixth century BC but his spiritual journey started when – as the Brahmin, Megha – he met Lord Dipankara 91 'incalculable aeons' earlier.

9 H. White, 'Indigenous Peoples, the International Trend Toward Legal Personhood for Nature, and the United States', *American Indian Law Review*, XLIII/1 (2018), pp. 129–65.

10 Some of the six days of creation in the hexameral tradition were even before the creation of the Sun and Earth, the existence of which, together, define the 24-hour day.

11 Of course, there is nothing inherently wrong in raising the dead. The biosphere is porous and forests' mycorrhizal partnerships, for example, demonstrate one completely sustainable way of accessing the Underworld's riches. In fact, the living must constantly raise the dead in order to survive.

12 It has been demonstrated that the oral tradition can effectively transmit the contents of such stories over thousands of years, for example, from the (archaeological) Bronze Age to the present day. See S. Graça da Silva and J. J. Tehrani, 'Comparative Phylogenetic Analyses Uncover the Ancient Roots of Indo-European Folktales', *Royal Society Open Science*, III/1 (2016), pp. 1–11.

13 Other collective responses could include diet. But what we choose to eat – meat or plant – is an integral part of our cultural identity. (After all, Pythagoras championed a plant-based diet out of respect for animals' Personhood, since they were the vehicles of his ancestors' souls.) And because the food we eat is so much more culturally laden than the fuel we put in our cars, a supposedly 'neutral and value-free' modern science that proudly eschews cultural entanglements is ill equipped to address the question.

14 In Japan in the seventh century AD, a day-to-day calendar was established by a *Ritsuryo* government bureau called *Onmyoryo*, which literally means 'yin-yang office'. The yin-yang office has no connection with the Western zodiac or calendar, but its existence suggests a

continuity between ancient sacred understandings of time and the modern secular understanding of time. The names of 24 *sekki* and 72 *kō* (approximately fifteen- and five-day-long mini-seasons, respectively) suggest an enduring connection with Nature. For example, 'Pure and clear' (5–19 April) consists of 'Swallows return' (5–9 April), 'Wild geese fly north' (10–14 April) and 'First rainbows' (15–19 April).

15 A. N. Whitehead called the whole of European philosophy a 'series of footnotes to Plato'. There are therefore many who take issue with Plato's constant, unchanging world of essences. One of the problems with the ideal Realm of Being is that it has encouraged some people to downgrade the Realm of Becoming. Some people have interpreted it as 'anti-nature' and used it to justify hostility towards life on Earth, including hostility to the other-than-human. However, this is not an issue for the traditional sciences, which acknowledge that neither pure form nor pure matter actually exists, and assume that the Realm of Becoming participates in the Realm of Being. Moreover, the traditional zodiac is not a philosophical system intent on tying up loose ends. It is, instead, an essentially practical aide-memoire that is open to life's mysteries.

BIBLIOGRAPHY

Albertus Magnus, *Book of Minerals*, trans. Dorothy Wyckoff (Oxford, 1967)
Apollodorus, *The Library of Greek Mythology*, trans. Robin Hard
 (Oxford, 2008)
Aristotle, *De Anima*, trans. Hugh Lawson-Tancred (London, 1987)
—, *History of Animals*, trans. D'Arcy Wentworth Thompson (London, 1907)
—, *Metaphysics*, trans. Hugh Lawson-Tancred (London, 1998)
Aubrey, John, *Brief Lives*, ed. Kate Bennett (Oxford, 2018)
Beowulf, trans. Seamus Heaney (London, 2000)
Bethada Náem nÉrenn, Lives of Irish Saints, ed. and trans. Charles Plummer,
 2 vols (Oxford, 1922)
Bible, King James Version
Blake, William, *The Complete Poems*, ed. Alicia Ostriker (London, 1977)
Bradford, William, *Of Plymouth Plantation, 1620–47*, ed. Samuel Eliot
 Morison (New Brunswick, NJ, 1952)
Browne, Thomas, *Urne Buriall and the Garden of Cyrus*, ed. John Carter
 (Cambridge, 2016)
Butler, Charles, *The Feminine Monarchie* (Farmington Hills, MI, 2018)
Chaucer, Geoffrey, *The Canterbury Tales*, trans. David Wright (Oxford, 2011)
Clare, John, *Major Works*, ed. Eric Robinson and David Powell
 (Oxford, 2008)
Claridge, John, *The Country Calendar* (London, 1946)
The Cloud of Unknowing, trans. Clifton Wolters (London, 1978)
Culpeper, Nicholas, *Culpeper's Complete Herbal* (London, 2009)
Dante Alighieri, *Divine Comedy*, trans. C. H. Sisson (Oxford, 1993)
Darwin, Charles, *Descent of Man*, ed. James Moore (London, 2004)
—, *The Formation of Vegetable Mould* (London, 1882)
Dick, Philip Kindred, *Do Androids Dream of Electric Sheep?* (New York,
 1996)
Drayton, Michael, *Works*, ed. John William Hebel, 5 vols (Oxford, 1931–41)
Emerson, Ralph Waldo, *Collected Poems and Translations*, ed. Harold Bloom
 and Paul Kane (New York, 1994)

Ernaux, Annie, *The Years* (London, 2018)

Ferguson, James, *Astronomy Explained upon Sir Isaac Newton's Principles* (London, 1794)

Goethe, Johann Wolfgang von, *Metamorphosis of Plants*, trans. Douglas Miller (Cambridge, MA, 2009)

Hardy, Godfrey Harold, *A Mathematician's Apology* (Cambridge, 1992)

Heraclitus, *Fragments*, trans. Brooks Haxton (London, 2003)

Homer, *Iliad*, trans. Emile Victor Rieu (London, 2003)

—, *Odyssey*, trans. Emile Victor Rieu (London, 2003)

Ibn Khaldûn, *Muqaddimah*, trans. Franz Rosenthal (Princeton, NJ, 2015)

Jacks, Lawrence Pearsall, *Mad Shepherds* (Oxford, 1979)

Jefferies, Richard, *The Game Keeper at Home* (Oxford, 1982)

Joyce, James, *Finnegans Wake* (London, 2000)

Keats, John, *The Complete Poems* (London, 1977)

Kerouac, Jack, *The Dharma Bums* (London, 2006)

Kimmerer, Robin Wall, *Braiding Sweetgrass* (London, 2013)

Larkin, Philip, *The Complete Poems*, ed. Archie Burnett (London, 2014)

Leopold, Aldo, *A Sand County Almanac* (New York, 1986)

Link, O. Winston, and Thomas Garver, *The Last Steam Railroad in America* (New York, 1995)

Linnaeus, Carl, *Philosophia Botanica*, trans. Stephen Freer (Oxford, 2005)

Lubbock, John, *Ants, Bees and Wasps*, ed. John Meyers (London, 1929)

Lucan, *The Civil War (Pharsalia)*, trans. J. D. Duff (Cambridge, MA, 1928)

Lucian of Samosata, *True History*, trans. Calum Maciver (New York, 2021)

Mandeville, Bernard, *The Fable of the Bees* (London, 1989)

Mann, Thomas, *The Magic Mountain*, trans. John E. Woods (New York, 1996)

Marvell, Andrew, *The Complete Poems*, ed. Elizabeth Donno (London, 2005)

Mintz, Sidney Wilfred, *Sweetness and Power* (New York, 1985)

Ovid, *Fasti*, trans. James G. Frazer (Cambridge, MA, 1931)

—, *Metamorphoses*, trans. Mary M. Innes (London, 1975)

Pepys, Samuel, *The Diary*, ed. Robert Latham and William Mathews (Berkeley, CA, 2000)

Plato, *Charmides. Alcibiades. Hipparchus. The Lovers. Theages. Minos. Epinomis*, trans. W.R.M. Lamb (Cambridge, MA, 1927)

—, *Republic*, trans. Desmond Lee (London, 1974)

—, *Timaeus and Critias*, trans. Desmond Lee (London, 1977)

Pliny the Elder, *Natural History*, trans. H. Rackham (London, 1968)

Porphyry, *On the Cave of the Nymphs*, trans. Thomas Taylor (London, 1917)

Rūmi, Jalaluddin, *The Mathnawī*, trans. Reynold A. Nicholson (London, 1926)

Shakespeare, William, *The Complete Works*, ed. Jonathan Bate and Eric Rasmussen (London, 2008)

Steinbeck, John, *Cannery Row* (London, 2000)
Tales from the Thousand and One Nights, trans. Nessim Joseph Dawood (Harmondsworth, 1973)
Theophrastus, *Enquiry into Plants*, trans. Arthur Hort (London, 1916)
Thoreau, Henry David, *The Journal: 1837–61*, ed. Damion Searls (New York, 2009)
—, *Walden; or, Life in the Woods* (London, 2017)
Tyson, Paul, *A Christian Theology of Science: Reimagining a Theological Vision of Natural Knowledge* (Grand Rapids, MI, 2022)
Virgil, *Aeneid VII–XII*, trans. Henry Rushton Fairclough, ed. G. P. Goold (Cambridge, MA, 2000)
—, *Eclogues; Georgics; Aeneid I–VI*, trans. Henry Rushton Fairclough (Cambridge, MA, 1986)
White, Gilbert, *The Natural History of Selborne*, ed. Anne Secord (Oxford, 2013)
White, Terence Hanbury, *The Book of Merlyn* (London, 2015)
Wordsworth, William, *The Collected Poems* (Ware, 1994)
Wu, Cheng'en, *The Journey to the West*, ed. and trans. Anthony C. Yu, 4 vols (Chicago, 1977–83)
—, *The Monkey and the Monk*, ed. and trans. Anthony C. Yu (Chicago, 2006)
Yates, Frances Amelia, *The Art of Memory* (London, 2014)
Yeats, William Butler, *Poems Selected by Seamus Heaney* (London, 2000)
The Yellow Book of Lecan, ed. Robert Atkinson (Dublin, 1896)
Zaleski, Carol, *Otherworld Journeys* (Oxford, 1987)

ACKNOWLEDGEMENTS

This book grew from an idea generously shared by Tchenka Jane Sunderland, whom I had met while looking for an astrologer to cast an expert eye over the manuscript of an earlier book, *Children of Mercury*. I was writing a book about how premodern artists may have understood the way their lives unfolded – following the 'Seven Ages' made famous by Shakespeare – and I needed someone well versed in traditional astrology to check my understanding of the planets. Over tea and biscuits at her kitchen table, towards the end of our discussions about the seven different planet-governed stages of life, Tchenka told me about some work she had undertaken a few years earlier.

Tchenka's idea had come to her over several decades, and its first inklings arose in response to hay fever. Recognizing that hay fever could occur any time between March and September, Tchenka realized that her own occurred in May–June, or Gemini, which is an air sign ruled by Mercury, the god of communication and exchange. She wondered whether the storm of pollen – vital to plants, but a cause of discomfort to some humans – could be considered a terrestrial manifestation of Mercury's aerial information transfer. Over time, more connections between natural phenomena and traditional star lore occurred to her and the jigsaw of the natural zodiac slowly assembled itself. The last pieces to fall into place were those associated with the winter months, when nature's activities are hidden under a cloak of darkness. She offered her findings in monthly weekend workshops that ran in the Norfolk countryside through 2015–16.

Through 2020–21, Tchenka very kindly sent her country workshop notes to me, month by month, allowing me to follow her ideas as I watched the year unfold. I came to appreciate her work as a piece of speculative – in the respectful, etymological sense of 'mirror-like' – natural history, attuned to the Aristotelian and Neoplatonic world with which I had become familiar through my own extensive research into the worldviews of historic European artists. I also saw in it a refreshingly different approach to ecology, one that suggested that, even if the immediate causes of our ecological crisis lie in the technologies spawned by modern science, the crisis has its roots in the modern West's metaphysical assumptions. (Metaphysical assumptions – which are inescapable – are extraordinarily powerful precisely because they are usually unquestioned. Paul Tyson's book, listed in the bibliography, provides an excellent historical account of our current Western metaphysic, how it developed from premodern metaphysics and what a postmodern Western metaphysic might look like.)

I took Tchenka's idea and ran with it, and, although she read manuscript versions and suggested revisions, all the errors are my own. Also, the choice of particular illustrative natural phenomena was mine alone, and many other ecologies – featuring different animals, vegetables, minerals and interactions – could also be written to exemplify the complex web of interconnected relationships implied by the zodiac's changing combinations of elements and planets.

I would like to thank Adam Bobbette, Patrick Curry, Ferdinand Saumarez Smith and Julian Yates most sincerely for their comments on the text. Again, all errors remain my own. I would also like to thank Claire Barnes for her encouragement, and Christine Kimbriel, Camille Polkownik, Charlotte Quirk and Camille Turner-Hehlen at Emil Tonka, as well as Ian Pittock at the University Library, Cambridge.

At Reaktion Books I would like to thank Alex Ciobanu and Martha Jay. And, once again, I would like to thank Michael Leaman for supporting my experiments in writing. My previous books have all been attempts to find different ways of writing about paintings and painters using, in particular, the knowledge that can flow from a painting conservation studio. This book has enabled me to take some lessons learned from a sympathetic engagement with historic artists' materials and methods, and apply them to another area of conservation, the conservation of nature. I am most grateful for that opportunity. I also hope that these writings might encourage others to engage respectfully with the premodern world with an eye to the postmodern world.

Finally, I want to express my profound thanks to my wife, Tara, for allowing this book to spread across much of our kitchen table for several years, as well as for reading and suggesting improvements to earlier versions, and for so much more.

All images and diagrams are the author's own.

INDEX